Veggies for Carnivores

Moving Vegetables to the Center of the Plate

LORA KRULAK

CHANGING LIVES PRESS

Changing Lives Press
50 Public Square #1600
Cleveland, OH 44113
www.changinglivespress.com

Library of Congress Cataloging-in-Publication Data is available through the Library of Congress.

Editor: Shari Johnson
Production: www.thebookcouple.com
Cover photo by Suki Zoe
Interior photographs by Rebecca Cobb

Printed in the United States of America

10   9   8   7   6   5   4   3   2   1

Contents

For my grandparents

Introduction

I remember the moment I realized that I didn't belong in Ohio. When I was 15 years old my mother, a traveler at heart, swept my two brothers and me off to Italy for a two-week holiday. First stop: Treviso, home of Benetton. Mind you, it was the mid-80s, and the Benetton Polo fashion phenomenon had not yet graced our shores.

I ventured out on my own, feeling confident in my suburban America-style *Madonna-esque* bob, thick eyebrows and white overalls. I sat on a bridge and watched the local kids in awe. I was envious of their style and suddenly self-conscious of my own. These kids were innately cool. They had style. They sat at cafés, drank little coffees, smoked cigarettes, drove Vespas, and made it effortlessly chic. A very handsome Italian boy approached me and said something in Italian. I must have stared at him bug-eyed and blankly because he just laughed. I was frozen. What on earth could I say to him? I didn't want him to think that I was an ignorant and unfashionable American—even though I had just realized that's what I was!

Flushed, I ran back to our hotel and resolved to spend the rest of our holiday studying Italians: the type of shoes they wore, the style of their jeans, what they ordered at cafés, and what they bought in the markets. I listened, and I observed. From that day forward, I have done that wherever I travel—I listen, and I observe.

To understand a culture is to understand how the people live—where they shop, what their ritual of tea or coffee is. One of my yoga teachers once said that if you want to learn what your guru knows, walk like him. I believe this is the essence of truly learning about a culture. And food is at the heart of it.

Markets are the epicenter of most cities and villages around the world. This is the core of where you can learn the most about a culture. I've spent hours shopping for spices, reading labels, asking vendors to translate and explain how the locals shop, what they bought, and why. This also helped accommodate my own particular eating habits, as I'd already discovered that certain foods didn't work well for me. I was able to learn what flours were gluten-free, what sugars were unrefined, and what cheeses were made from goat or sheep milk.

At the time, food allergies and intolerances were not on the radar of the dietary mainstream, nor a topic readily discussed. Cutting out wheat, dairy, and refined sugar from the diet was not anything considered "normal" and certainly not done at most restaurants. Fortunately, when I began making these dietary changes in my early twenties I had already moved to Manhattan, New York, a melting pot of gastronomic cultures. I began taking cooking classes, reading books, and substituting ingredients that didn't agree with me for ones that did. Food intolerances taught me to experiment and to explore the global flavors and exotic spices that had so inspired me.

Everywhere I traveled, I asked a few more questions of the locals and learned a little bit more about the importance of spices, herbs, seasonings, and freshness. Through my trials and experiments, I became a rare mix of culinary adventurer and dietary problem solver. As I sought to decode my own nutritional riddles, I came to understand how to do that for others.

From India to Bali, Australia to Thailand, I sought balance in studies of yoga, nutrition, herbology, and even chocolate. Not satisfied with simply conquering my own nutritional challenges, I was determined to make this knowledge available to anyone in need of this guidance. "Easy and accessible" became my bywords, and I moved on to work one-on-one with private clients from around the world, helping to set them on their own individual paths to wellness.

A client once called me an artist with a blender and a basket of vegetables. This art school degree I received so long ago has proven itself useful.

Veggies For Carnivores™ is a glimpse at my culinary style and at how I see the world. It is a foray into global kitchens and how I translate them. It's been an extraordinary journey so far, but this is only where the adventure begins.

Bon voyage and bon appetite!

—Lora

CHAPTER ONE

The Basics

One of the longest and most consistent relationships I have had in my life is with vegetables. I have traveled the world visiting local markets, sneaking into local kitchens, befriending local cooks. Along the way I asked a lot of questions. With each encounter and in each country I learned something new from my reliable and organic-loving friends who romanced my palate and led me toward a new way to approach cooking. Taking on the task of creating healthy and delicious food turned out to be a lot easier than I thought. However, despite the piles of beautifully colored, gleaming, organic vegetables displayed in our markets, people gravitate toward the same choices again and again. We tend to be creatures of habit and convenience, and the sight of a celery root or a pile of unidentifiable leafy greens can be intimidating—even though our adventurous, Food TV–addicted side is arguing for us to try something new.

Now honestly, how much microwaved-steamed broccoli can a person eat? It is just as easy and a lot more compelling to wilt some greens, toss them with olive oil, and a sprinkle of *lime-chili-salt* created with pantry ingredients. My mission is to demystify vegetables and show the world how sexy they are. They are more than just side dishes—they are worthy of center stage.

Experience has taught me that vegetables are not just something your mother made you eat—they are delicious, elementary to prepare, and a joy to eat. My goal in writing *Veggies for Carnivores* is to celebrate the flavors, health benefits, and, yes, the beauty of vegetables.

Veggies For Carnivores™ is my straightforward approach to cooking extraordinarily tasting, healthy food that can be incorporated into every dish and every diet for every person. The concept is that anyone can cook luscious, healthy food any time, anywhere, and in any kitchen. Basic building blocks and components will allow the reader to mix and match to suit individual palates and maximize the bounty of the season. All that is needed are some *fundamental* local ingredients, a few simple tools, and a small repertoire of sauces to use as building blocks for dressings, marinades, toppings, sides, and even dips.

The recipes are uncomplicated, easy to follow, and laced with stories and antics from my travels around the world. The Ginger Lime Tonic was created with the help of the "Nimbu Pane Walla" (lemonade man) who had a stand right by my apartment in New Delhi. I loved his brew, but requested he make it for me with honey instead of sugar. I was obsessed with the Crunchy Nut Brittle inspired by the snack man in Istanbul who showed me the secrets of this sticky concoction of nuts and seeds. I stood outside his shop every day for a week, peering in the window, watching him mix the nuts and the seeds in a seemingly effortless manner. He finally invited me in for a quick lesson on how to make it. I had to roll up my creative sleeves for that one to omit the 6 or 7 pounds of sugar in the original recipe.

The recipes in *Veggies for Carnivores* utilize mainly citrus fruit, vegetables, and herbs, although meat or fish may be added for variation. The recipes are comprised of simple techniques that allow the natural flavors of real food to shine. The result will create healthier cravings and new habits—not to mention more delicious, nutritious, exciting meals and moments.

A FEW TIPS ON USING THIS BOOK

I prefer to teach a *technique,* such as blending, freezing, slicing, or chopping, as opposed to just following a recipe. Once learned, you can then use the technique to design countless dishes using favorite, seasonal ingredients. Although I encourage learning to judge by eye and by taste, I have provided exact measures for each recipe. I like to teach cooking by taste, as it expands the palate and the mind. Learning to run with a recipe is easier than it looks; you will be able to create your own dishes by not depending on measuring spoons and cups. Please improvise, play, experiment, and let me know if your version is better or you have come up with an entirely new way of going about the recipe. Follow your senses of taste, smell, sight, and even touch, but most of all, have fun.

You will see that I encourage improvising by suggesting substitute ingredients such as trying arugula, lime, and walnuts instead of basil and pine nuts for the pesto. Adding more liquid or less liquid immediately changes the recipe from a dressing to a dip, or vice versa.

Recipe Re Deux, a.k.a. Substitutes— Understanding How to Use Alternate Ingredients

When I arrive in a new city or new country, chances are my first stop will be the local market. This is how I raise my comfort level and get my bearings. For me it's a glimpse into how the locals eat and live. Straight off the plane from New York to Jerusalem a few summers ago, I dropped my bags at the hotel and immediately headed to the Mahane Yehuda Market. Fortunately it was Friday afternoon, the height of market day and the place was buzzing with excitement. I walked into one shop that was overflowing with people who were grabbing one particular dessert that appeared to be chocolate rugulah. I don't eat rugulah, but a sweet man wearing a chocolate-covered apron saw me staring in awe and disbelief at all of the people. He asked me why I looked surprised as he handed me a warm pastry.

"Is it always this crowded?" I asked the man as I took his little gift of rugulah and put it in my bag to save for later. He nodded, laughed, and said that he would set some aside for me as they would sell out in about an hour. This pastry tasted like melted, warm chocolate, and I honestly nearly lost my footing when I tasted it. It was that good. I went back and bought a box of them.

Middle Eastern food is an excellent illustration of how the Veggies For Carnivores™ concept works. With just a few subtle twists, an entirely new dish is created from seemingly the same ingredients. Halva is a great example. It is made with ground sesame seeds, sugar, and a bit of salt. Add some chocolate, and it's a fresh, innovative dish. Remove the sugar, and it is tahini. Add some chickpeas and it is hummus. Use maple syrup instead of sugar, and it's now free of refined sugar. The creations are endless, all from a simple base of sesame seeds and olive oil.

Every culture has its staples, but staples are comparable every-where you go. Like people, they may look different on the outside, but at the core they are all quite similar. Let's say you have a group of old friends who know each other well. They know what to expect from each other and how to relate to one another. But if one of the group is suddenly substituted by a stranger, that person could have physical similarities but the interactions of the group would shift slightly because of the addition of the new element. So it is with food and ingredients. For example, if I have no maple or *yacon* syrup (explained in detail in the Base Ingredients section) because I am in the middle of Jordan, I can use date syrup to get the sweet-ness I need and create a new dish because the subtle twist in flavor will affect the relationship of the other ingredients to one another. Thus, wherever you are, you can count on finding your base ingre-dients. I always veer toward the most natural and pure ingredient I can find, but when stumped I can dig myself out of a hole with a local substitution.

BASE INGREDIENTS

Sweeteners—Coconut sugar (also called palm sugar), molasses, honey, or maple syrup (sometimes date or yacon)

Veggies and Veggie remnants—These are the leftover parts you were going to throw away.

Herbs—Any herb, any color, dried or fresh

Oil—Cold pressed and organic is best (mainly olive oil, coconut oil, sesame oil, flaxseed oil, hemp oil, and avocado oil)

Salt—A good salt is key. I normally use Himalayan or Celtic but a good grey sea salt, sel de mer, or fleur de sel will do, as they are rich in sea minerals and iodine.

Acid—Limes, lemons, orange, apple cider vinegar, or ume plum vinegar and sometimes an occasional balsamic

Sweeteners

My five top sweeteners currently are:

1. **Yacon Syrup**—This subtle sweetener is a high source of FOS (fructooligosaccharide) and friendly bacteria. Its taste is similar to molasses and caramel. Yacon is a South American root that is slightly sweet and similar in taste to a Jerusalem artichoke or a jicama, but sweeter. It can be made into a powder or syrup and used as a glycemic sweetener.

2. **Maple Syrup**—It is on the mellow side of sweet and can be heated or used cold. Maple dissolves easily and blends well with sweet or savory. I do prefer an organic maple and love the taste of the darker syrups, so I will normally buy a U.S. Grade B from Upstate New York. However, ask the producer or at the shop where you are buying it, because most classifications of grades differ, depending on where it is from.

3. **Honey**—I prefer a raw honey. Honey yields a significant flavor in savory dishes and dressings and is a good choice for smoothies. However, I don't like to heat honey as heat removes most of the beneficial antimicrobial properties and the friendly bacteria. A small amount of cooked honey isn't going to hurt you, but a bit of raw honey can help you a lot.

4. **Molasses**—It's high in iron, potassium, and magnesium and has a subtle internal cleansing effect. Molasses cooks well and is magnificent in desserts.

5. **Coconut Sugar/Palm Sugar**—From the tropics, this sugar is easily substituted for brown sugar or demura sugar. Its low glycemic index makes it superb for diabetics and its subtle taste enables it to be quite the chameleon.

Honey and white sugar can, of course, be found almost anywhere in the world. However, with a little digging, there are many other delicious local sweeteners to choose from.

Useful Facts about Global Sweeteners

India—Sugar is in almost everything you could eat or drink in India. Sugar is often referred to as a poor man's protein—but that does not always refer to the white, processed, Domino kind. Southern India has one of my favorite forms of sugar, called jaggery. It is an unrefined, unprocessed sweetener that is a deep, rich, caramel color; its taste resembles that of molasses. Jaggery can be made from coconut, date, or sugarcane and is often a combination of all three. It has a very high mineral content, and some Ayruvedic doctors prescribe it for stomachaches or "sore thoughts."

Middle East—Delicious pure honey and date syrup are in nearly everything. Date syrup is thick, smoothly sweet, and, like jaggery, it resembles molasses. Although the iron content is not as high in date syrup as it is in molasses, it is a good "supplemental" source of iron and other valuable minerals.

Asia—Has some deliciously curious sugars. I love brown rice syrup and use it often in baking. It acts almost like healthy glue by binding foods together well and easily replaces white sugar.

South East Asia and Indonesia—Coconut sugar is straight from the coconut with a flavor, again, closer to molasses but much sweeter. Palm sugar, made from the center of the palm tree, yields a very similar taste and is often substituted for coconut sugar or vice versa. Most often they are labeled as the same.

South America—This may not belong here because Stevia is found almost everywhere now, although it has many other commercial names. However, it is a plant indigenous to Paraguay and does not raise the glycemic index at all, so it is a perfect sweetener for diabetics or those following a sugar-free diet. Stevia can be a bit bitter, but it's a nice option and is available in health food shops and most supermarkets.

AYURVEDIC MEDICINE

Ayurvedic medicine is an ancient Indian holistic science of health and longevity. The philosophy is centered on healing the whole person—body, mind, and spirit. Each diagnosis is dependent upon the individual and his or her constitution. Diet is essential in Ayurvedic medicine, and food is a large component of the *prescription*. Particular spices, teas, foods, and food combinations are all prescribed by the Ayurvedic doctor.

Acids

Citrus—(My acid of choice.) Most every culture has limes. Lemons are much more American and are technically a local form of a lime. **Limes** yield a sweeter flavor than **lemons** and pair well with nearly everything. Lemons, as we know, tend to be a bit sour. I interchange lemons and limes without thought. Sometimes the more thought you put into it, the less fun you're going to have—and the greater chance for boredom. Just play. Much like learning a new language, it is the best way to learn. If you have no lemons or limes, an **orange** or a **grapefruit** will work brilliantly.

Vinegar—I use **apple cider vinegar** often. It has a delicate flavor that interacts well with other ingredients. Cider vinegar is not as fermented as most vinegars and is excellent for the digestive system as well as for burning fat.

However, there is a multitude of delicious vinegars to choose from. A few that I like to use are **ume plum vinegar** from Japan, which is also fantastic for the digestive system, and **balsamic**. If I use balsamic, I will use only a smidgen. I learned this from an Italian friend who showed me that when using balsamic, the ratio of oil to the vinegar should be about 15 to 1! Go figure.

Oil

Every culture has an oil that is used most often. Some oils are better than others for given roles, but most have nutritional value.

Olive oil—The oil I use most often is olive oil. It is pure, clean, and healthful. It does, however, have a very low burning point. When cooking with it, add a pinch of coconut oil or organic butter to raise the burning point.

Coconut oil—Coconut oil is indigenous to India, Asia, and Indonesia. These cultures have been cooking with it for thousands of years. It is cheap, healthy, and versatile. Its antimicrobial properties make it a natural parasite killer and digestive aid. Further, it's a thyroid stimulator and an anti-aging nutrient. I love using the oil because of its high burning point. Coconut oil is found in suntan lotions because it contains natural sunscreen properties and moisturizes the skin. Bruce Fife's book *The Coconut Oil Miracle* contains a full explanation on all its uses and benefits.

Salt

I LOVE SALT. This may be my next book: *Passions for Salt*. A vast array of salts awaits you, depending on the flavor or benefit desired. The health benefits of **Himalayan salt** and **Celtic sea salt** are astounding. The sea minerals in them help the body absorb the nutrients and minerals it needs as well as enhance the flavor of the food. A good salt will not just make the food taste "salty." I have friends in Bali who developed a flaked sea salt that comes packaged inside of a coconut shell, which I think is so clever. It's deliciously sweet, light, and melts when put in food. This is similar to the effects of **Maldon** flaked salt from the UK, which is another fine sea salt.

NECESSARY EQUIPMENT

BLENDER BASICS

People often ask which they should invest in—a blender or a food processor. I always vote for the blender, as I am partial to a smooth purée and this requires a strong machine. Blenders are easy to clean and require little maintenance. In addition to purée, a blender can emulsify, which is useful for dressings and sauces; blend for smoothies, drinks, and soups; and grind or chop bread-crumbs, ice, and even herbs. As the barrel is narrow on most machines, more liquid is normally required. Therefore, blenders are not the best choice for dough. There are a few models, such as the Vitamix® or the Blendtec®, that do have a wide container. If you are a baker, you can actually make a dough in either of these machines, although I would not recommend it.

My enthusiasm for the blender began when I discovered the

world of raw foods and took my first raw food cooking class with my dear friend Renee Loux. The raw foodists used the blender, mostly the Vitamix®, to make almost everything. All of the soups, smoothies, and sauces were blended in the powerful machine. This influenced my cooking more than anything up to that point.

When it comes to choosing the right blender, there are a few things to keep in mind:

1. Never, and I repeat, never buy a blender that has a screw-on bottom. The chances of losing your liquid and creating a mess are very high.

2. The blades should be positioned at different angles. This enables the machine to give you a smooth purée as well as chop tougher ingredients such as ice or root vegetables.

3. A larger jar or barrel is best for scooping out ingredients, therefore making for easier cleanup.

In my opinion, the two best blenders on the market are the Vitamix® and the Blendtec®. They are pricey, but if you calculate the per-use cost for cost ratio, it pays for itself rather quickly. My machine has paid for itself several times over. Cleanup is easy. You can make nut butters, soups, bread batter, and even guacamole. They have adjusting speeds and when it comes to making smooth smoothies or soups, there is no comparison. Both of these brands can handle hot liquids, which is important if you plan to make soups because hot liquids can cause the top on a blender to *explode*. The capacity jar is also very large.

Blenders

KitchenAid®—This is a powerful machine. KitchenAid® has made the best mixers for a very long time, and I am now fond of their blenders. Its five-speed model works similarly to a variable speed blender. The blades are positioned well and the jar is wide enough to insert your mixing tool for poking and stirring food that gets caught at the bottom. The jar is heavy enough not to rattle and make ghastly noises.

Viking®—These are superb machines that blend and purée well, but they don't chew the veggie pieces completely and will require additional liquid. However, they are quality, solid machines that will give you little or no trouble.

Waring®—Named for the owner of the company and big band leader, Fred Waring, they have been making blenders for over sixty years. Waring makes the standard narrow bar blender often seen in nightclubs and bars. Cleanup is easy, and they work very well, but much like the Viking, more liquid is needed to get a smooth purée. These are not good machines for dips or butters, but fine for soups and dressings, and they are exceptionally good for smoothies, tonics, or elixirs.

Cuisinart®—Honestly, one can't go wrong buying a Cuisinart. They make a mean blender with several different models to choose from. The blades are sharp and can crush veggie remnants without having to add extra liquid. My only issue with the Cuisinart is the screw-on bottom.

FOOD PROCESSORS

Food processors can be very useful. Most models have interchangeable blades and disks and are excellent for quick shredding, grating, slicing, chopping, and even for kneading dough. They will cream a soup, but the purée will never be as smooth as it would be if a blender were used.

The smaller food processors are excellent for chopping herbs or quickly grinding nuts and seeds. If I had to choose, I would invest in a solid blender and a small food processor.

MANDOLINE

Nothing can compare to a mandoline for fast, perfect slicing and shredding. They are inexpensive, very useful tools to have in your kitchen that can prove to be irreplaceable. I will repeat my warnings later in the book, but I don't think one can be too cautious in the kitchen. Use the hand guard or a towel when slicing. Fingertips may heal, but it's not worth going through the pain. I know! These tools are sharp and for good reason.

There is no need to spend a lot of money when purchasing a mandoline; sometimes the more expensive ones are not as good. I find that V shaped or angle blade is good for slicing.

Here are my three favorites, and I actually own and use all of them:

1. **OXO**—This is my top tier model and does everything necessary that a mandoline should. It has V-shaped blades and can slice and shred clean veggies every time. It also has a good hand guard.

2. **Benriner Japanese Mandoline Slicer**—This is a basic model that can be bought on Amazon for about $20. It has all of the pieces necessary for shredding and julienning as well as slicing.

3. **Kyocera Ceramic Slicer**—This one only slices. It was a gift and I fell in love with it. It's perfect for slicing fennel or squash and making an all green salad. Again, please note, very sharp blade!

CHAPTER TWO

Oil-Based Sauces and Dressings

Sauces, dips, dressings, and spreads are the building blocks for the Veggies for Carnivores™ approach. The consistent theme and formula to remember is to start with a **dried** or **fresh herb**; a **vegetable** or a **vegetable remnant**; a **blender** (a food processor will work as well); a good-quality **olive oil** (or oil of choice; **lemon** or **lime** (or your choice of an **acid**); and a good-quality **salt**. The sauces, dips, dressings, and spreads in the first chapters are variations on this theme with the key difference being the **quantity of oil or liquid** used to create the right consistency and desired flavor. If I am making a dip, I will add less oil or water to an already existing dressing recipe so that I am left with a thick creamy dip. If I want a sauce, let's say for pasta, I'll use a moderate amount of oil so it's the perfect consistency. There is no reason why a salad dressing wouldn't be fabulous on pasta, rice, or quinoa.

Once you have the basic formula down, there are limitless creations to be made. Perhaps you have the ingredients for salad dressing but no blender. You can make the same dressing recipe chunky and call it chutney or simply use it as a side dish. I encourage you to be creative and fearless. To me, cooking is a moving meditation; it's not serious, other than when chopping—at which time keeping your eyes open is most certainly required.

Each sauce and dressing can be used on pretty much any green, any salad, or really anything you feel it pairs well with. I will suggest some pairings, but this chapter is comprised of a very versatile group of sauces and dressings with the flexibility to mix and match.

Recipes Included in This Chapter

Fennel Top and Shallot Dressing

Sweet Avocado Dressing

The Basic Pesto

Carrot Ginger Dressing

Lemony Tarragon Dressing

Miso, Tahini, and Scallion Dressing

Sweet Basil Dressing

Limey Mint Vinaigrette

Sweet Basil Corn Dressing

Tomato Basil Dressing

Garlicky Red Pepper Sauce

Sun-dried Tomato and Olive Sauce

Sun-dried Tomatoes and Cashewed
Thousand Island Sauce

Fennel Top and Shallot Dressing

One spring, my friend Lulu and I were staying in her new apartment in the Trastevere district of Rome. We did not have a fridge, so were forced to buy fresh ingredients daily and use what we had quickly and efficiently. Fennel is abundant in the spring in Italy, and Lulu and I ate a lot of it. I felt horrid about throwing the arms and fronds away, so I tried to eat them like carrots, but the stringiness bothered me. We did have a blender so I tossed all of the extra fennel parts together and a new dressing emerged.

INGREDIENTS

Tops of one fennel, roughly chopped

Bunch of flat leaf Italian parsley, ripped into pieces
(or herbs of choice)

1 lime, juiced

1 shallot, roughly chopped

Big pinch roasted garlic

Splash of nama shoyu or soy sauce
(tamari for gluten free)

Splash of maple syrup

2 to 3 cups olive oil
(can supplement with part veggie broth)

$1/4$ cup water to thin (optional)

Salt and pepper to taste

1. Place all of the ingredients into a blender, except the olive oil.

2. Turn the blender on low and slowly drizzle the oil in.

3. Add more oil or water for a thinner dressing.

4. Add salt and pepper to taste.

Sweet Avocado Dressing

I never truly appreciated the avocado until I lived in Australia. The Aussies use it in a multitude of ways that I had never imagined. The Byron-Bay special breakfast was gluten-free pumpkin toast with honey, tahini, and avocado. This was oddly delicious and as close to a perfect breakfast as I have ever had. One day I put some lettuce on top, and I started thinking about how the sweetness of the honey alters the taste of the avocado. When I was back stateside, I tried it with maple syrup. This dressing is outrageous on salads, as the avocado acts more as a cream-a-fier than a taste determiner, and it's often unrecognizable.

INGREDIENTS

$1/2$ to 1 whole avocado

1 lime or small lemon

1 to 1 $1/2$ cups high-quality olive oil

1 tsp. maple syrup

1 tsp. nama shoyu, soy sauce, or tamari

Salt and pepper to taste

1. Toss the avocado, lime, maple, and nama shoyu in the blender.

2. Turn blender on low and slowly drizzle the olive oil into the blender, emulsifying ingredients.

3. The dressing should be thick but can be thinned out with a bit of water or a bit more olive oil.

4. Add salt and pepper to taste.

To Adjust the Flavor

- Nama shoyu or tamari can be increased for a deeper, richer flavor.

- The maple syrup can be increased or decreased to satisfy sweet or savory desires.

If the avocados are not in season and do not taste flavorful to you, add more nama shoyu and maple syrup to beef up the flavors.

FASCINATING FACT

If your avocado is not ripe, put it in a paper bag on the counter for a day or so. This speeds up the ripening process.

The Basic "Pesto"

For versatility, I don't use cheese or nuts in my pesto, so I guess it's not a veritable pesto but more of a "green dressing." No matter. It tastes great and is a platform for many delicious variations. Change the herb to whatever you really crave or whatever's on hand to use. I've used straight parsley because that's all I had. Also, if you don't have orange, use all lemon, or mix lemon and lime. Play, have fun, and make it your own.

INGREDIENTS

1 orange, juiced

Zest of 1 orange

4 Tbsp. lemon juice (about 1 small lemon)

Splash of nama shoyu, soy sauce, or tamari for gluten free

1–2 bunches of cilantro, chopped

Good-quality olive oil

1 clove garlic, smashed (optional)

1. Mix all of the ingredients in a blender, except the olive oil.

2. Slowly drizzle the oil in and blend until smooth and desired thickness. (This dressing should be on the thinner side.)

3. Add salt and pepper to taste.

VARIATIONS

- Replace the cilantro with mint, parsley, spinach, or tarragon.

- Toss a handful of raw pine nuts, walnuts, or almonds into the blender.

- For carnivores, add parmesan or pecorino cheese!

Carrot Ginger Dressing

I credit this to my glamorous friend Allison, who was also my inspiration to go to cooking school . . . finally. She and I were early admirers of the famous chef Jean-Georges and his Asian twists. She introduced me to his ginger dressing, and it has been evolving ever since. The addition of the ume plum adds a depth and kick that I find is missing from a lot of ginger dressings. This is also scrumptious as a sandwich spread.

INGREDIENTS

2 medium sized carrots, roughly chopped

1 tsp. ume plum* or 1 Tbsp. ume plum paste

1 small lemon, juiced

2 tsp. nama shoyu or tamari sauce

2 tsp. coconut sugar or 1 tsp. honey

1-inch piece of ginger, pealed

$1/2$ small red onion

$1/2$ tsp. red chili powder

Pinch of cumin

1 cup olive oil

$1/8$ cup (or more) water to thin

Salt and pepper to taste

Ume plum or plum vinegar can be found in most good health food shops in the Asian section.

1. Chop the carrots into 1-inch pieces.

2. Toss in blender with the next eight ingredients.

3. Turn the blender on low, increasing to high and slowly drizzle the olive oil in.

4. Add salt and pepper to taste.

5. To thin the dressing, slowly drizzle the water in, up to $1/8$ cup.

Lemony Tarragon Dressing

Tarragon is an herb that I don't seem to tire of. The phase began when I had to make a dressing while in a friend of a friend's kitchen in the culinary wastelands of Upstate New York. All that was available were the few spices in the pantry, and the following recipe is what I came up with. Since that time, I have tried tarragon on everything from vegetables to steak. Tarragon is a marvelously fragrant herb that seems be exiled to French cooking only.

INGREDIENTS

Juice of 1 lemon

1 cup olive oil

3 Tbsp. dried tarragon or half a bunch fresh tarragon, roughly chopped (or ripped)

Splash of water

Large pinch of truffle salt (if you don't have or don't eat mushrooms, just omit and add regular salt)

2 tsp. apple cider vinegar

Splash of nama shoyu, soy sauce, or tamari for gluten free

1. Put all the ingredients in a blender.

2. Purée well and adjust salt according to taste.

A Carnivore's Choice

- This recipe is also a great marinade for a fish or even meat.

Miso, Tahini, and Scallion Dressing

I had the pleasure of working on a delightful spa book, *Asia's Ultimate Spas* by Judy Chapman. We shot photos for the book all over Bali, Thailand, and India. Bali is a popular destination for Japanese tourists, and as a result, miso has become a common cooking ingredient. Judy and I became fond of miso soup while we were shooting, as we found it grounding, soothing, and calming in our busy shooting schedule. In other words, it helped us to feel like our feet were again planted on earth. I suggest keeping miso paste as a staple in your fridge at all times. It is perfect for those days when you feel like your feet aren't touching the ground; it's soothing for a stomachache; and a teaspoon even works well for alleviating a hangover.

INGREDIENTS

2 Tbsp. miso

5–6 scallions, trimmed

2 Tbsp. tahini

1 Tbsp. chili powder

Juice of 1 lime

1 Tbsp. apple cider vinegar

1. Mix all ingredients together in a bowl or a blender.
2. Let sit to *rest* and marinate before tossing on anything.

FASCINATING FACT

Scallions have distinctively white and green parts. The white part is sweeter, softer, and tastes more like a shallot. The green part is sharper, grassier, and works best as a garnish. When cooked, the white part gets sweet and smooth and the green can get mushy if overcooked.

Sweet Basil Dressing

Similar to The Basic Pesto, I suppose this wouldn't be classified as a traditional pesto, so hence the name "sweet basil dressing."

INGREDIENTS

1 bunch basil, washed and de-stemmed

The reserved fronds and stems from the fennel bulb

$3/4$ cup high-quality extra virgin olive oil

$1/2$ freshly squeezed lemon juice

1 tsp. maple or honey (optional—depending on the desired outcome; do you want sweet or savory?)

White pepper and salt to taste

1. Place the basil, lemon, and maple or honey in a blender.

2. Turn blender on, starting slow and increasing speed to high and slowly drizzle the olive oil into the blender, emulsifying the ingredients.

3. The dressing will be thick. You can thin with a bit of water or a bit more olive oil.

4. Add salt and pepper to taste.

Limey Mint Vinaigrette

I led a very comfortable life during my time in New Delhi. I lived at the house of my friend's parents and, for most of the time, was cared for by their staff of many. Kumar, the very charming cook, made me the most refreshing lime-mint tonic every morning. Traditionally this drink would have been made with just lime, sugar, and water—but he and I worked on it and came up with this: He hand-pressed the mint into the lime rind to let the oils release and then mixed honey and jaggery into the paste. The paste was then mixed with water or soda. In the mornings he made it sweet and in the afternoons he added salt to make it more hydrating. (This recipe is in the tonic section.) The paste inspired this very refreshing dressing and can be made with or without sweetener.

INGREDIENTS

1 handful fresh mint leaves

2 Tbsp. lime juice

1 Tbsp. lemon juice

2 Tbsp. lime zest

1 small shallot, roughly chopped

1 tsp. Dijon mustard

$1/2$ tsp. maple syrup

Large pinch of good salt

1. Place all of the ingredients in a blender on high and blend away.

Sweet Basil Corn Dressing

This lovely sauce was devised in the height of summer when corn is at its sweetest. I had a lot of freshly picked corn (please note the Fascinating Fact box) and tossed it in. It was a heavenly outcome. This is a variation on the Sweet Basil Dressing—the only difference is the corn.

INGREDIENTS

1 bunch basil, washed and de-stemmed

$3/4$ cup high-quality extra virgin olive oil

$1/2$ cup freshly squeezed lemon juice

1 ear of corn, cut off the cob

White pepper and salt to taste

1. Place the corn into a medium-sized saucepan of boiling salted water for about 3 minutes.

2. Remove and strain well.

3. Toss the basil, lemon, and $1/2$ the corn in a blender.

4. Turn blender on low and increase speed, slowly drizzling the olive oil into the blender to emulsify.

5. The dressing will be thick and can be thinned with a bit of water or a bit more olive oil.

FASCINATING FACT

Corn turns to starch as soon as it is picked. If you have the pleasure of picking the corn yourself or even picking from your market, put it in a wet paper bag and put that bag inside a plastic bag and put it in the fridge. This almost stops the conversion process, making the corn taste and digest better.

Tomato Basil Dressing

This is the quintessential summer dressing in both flavor and texture. To me, summer is all about light, fresh, quick and easy, and truly letting the flavors shine on their own without much tinkering. Tomatoes are sweet, basil is smooth, and you pretty much can't go wrong. Fortunately, there is an abundance of types of tomatoes to choose from, and although best when in season, you can get them all year round.

FASCINATING FACT

Something I learned from an Italian friend who loves tomatoes: For some reason, tomatoes get sweeter when they are blended and turn the most beautiful shade of pink, which just so happens to be my favorite color.

INGREDIENTS

1 small box organic sweet grape tomatoes
(or the tomato of your choice)

Handful of basil

Pinch of crushed red pepper

Pinch of cinnamon

Salt and pepper to taste

1. Toss all of the ingredients in a blender and fire away.

2. Adjust the seasoning as needed.

FASCINATING FACT

Tomatoes don't like to be put in the fridge; please keep them on the counter.

SAUCES

Garlicky Red Pepper Sauce

I would LOVE to take full credit for this recipe, but my dear friend Mike Perrine—who has one of the most evolved palates I have ever witnessed—taught me this and it has since evolved and evolved. There are a few brilliant pieces of education in this simple sauce that can be used elsewhere and in other ways. For example, the sauce itself can be used as a pasta sauce, a vegetable sauce, or a warm salad dressing, and I have had friends who preferred it as a soup! The roasted garlic can be used as a spread for vegetables, for bread, or even melted on top of quinoa.

INGREDIENTS

3–4 red peppers, de-seeded,
cut into pieces and steamed or blanched

1–2 heads garlic, roasted

Bunch of chopped parsley or other herbs

Roughly chopped black olives

Sea salt

Juice of 1 lemon

1. Rub the garlic cloves with olive oil, wrap in tin foil, and roast at 375 degrees for about an hour or until soft. When the garlic is soft to the touch, remove from oven and let cool.

2. Heat a pot of salted, boiling water and blanch the peppers for about 4 minutes. Remove from the water and rinse with cool water to stop the cooking of the peppers.

3. Cut off the tops of the garlic and squeeze from the clove.

4. Place the peppers, salt, lemon, and garlic in a blender, starting slow and increasing speed. Begin to drizzle oil slowly into the mixture until completely smooth.

5. Stir in the chopped olives and the herbs.

VARIATIONS

- Tasty thing to do with this sauce—use it as a sauce for pizza.

- Use the roasted garlic on its own or as a spread for bread or a dip for chips.

FASCINATING FACT

Red peppers turn a gorgeous shade of pink after a short spin in the blender.

Sun-dried Tomato and Olive Sauce

There is a tradition in Italy of *Aperitivo*—to go for drinks before dinner. The bars present enormous buffets of snacks that could serve as a whole meal. When I was studying Italian in Rome with my friend Lulu, our favorite place to go was a bar called Enoteca Tri Luzzi. The bartender was a lovely woman named Fulvia, who often made fun of how I (literally) picked apart and merged different snack plates to suit my taste. One of the toppings on the focaccia was a sun-dried tomato pesto and another was straight black olive. Together they made a perfect dip for the roasted fennel that I spread them on. It seemed logical to me (and so foreign to Fulvia), but she soon gave up reprimanding me and laughed as she rearranged the food on the snack plates to cover all the *holes* I made while concocting my own versions.

INGREDIENTS

1 cup sun-dried tomatoes
soaked in fresh olive oil
for at least 1 hour or overnight,
at room temperature

$1/2$ cup chopped black olives

1 tsp. capers, chopped

$1/2$ cup olive oil

Juice of 1 lemon

1. Drain the tomatoes from the oil—reserving the oil for the sauce.

2. Roughly chop the tomatoes and mix with the olives and capers.

3. Whip together the oils and the lemon.

4. Mix all of the ingredients together and serve with bread, on a salad, or use as a topping for grilled salmon, steak . . . anything!

Sun-dried Tomatoes and Cashewed Thousand Island Sauce

While visiting an old friend in Ohio, we had a nostalgic conversation about the Thousand Island dressing and iceberg lettuce of our youth. After a few too many glasses of wine, we decided that we MUST have the salad, or a version of it. Unfortunately, we were in the middle of the culinary wastelands of America and the only shop open at 11 p.m. was a nameless all-night grocery store. Of course they did sell Miracle Whip, but neither of us was going to eat it. However, I found some sun-dried tomatoes at the store and had a brainstorm on a thickener. Cashews! We chopped up some celery to replace the relish and ate most of the dressing without the lettuce.

INGREDIENTS

5 or 6 sun-dried tomatoes soaked in olive oil

1 large handful of raw cashews

$1/4$ cup apple cider vinegar

1 to 2 cups olive oil

Pinch of crushed red pepper

Water to thin

35

1. After the tomatoes are soft, toss them into the blender (oil and all) with the cashews and the cider vinegar.

2. Slowly drizzle the extra olive oil into the blender with the blender on low, increasing speed.

3. Add salt and pepper to taste.

CHAPTER THREE

Thick Dips and Spreads

Dips and spreads are a staple in my diet. I often make a meal out of a few dips alongside a plate of crudité (raw vegetables). These are the opposite of an average spread such as mustard or mayo that would be the buffers or fillers for a meat or patty sandwich; these dips and spreads are the actual focal point and really need not much else to go with them—although they make a delicious topper for a protein or any vegetable.

The dips are all veggie-based and very concentrated. Meaning, a little bit goes a long way. They can be used in much the same way as the sauces and dressings, but used more sparingly.

Recipes Included in This Chapter

Edamame Dip

Roasted Garlic and Tomato Spread

Roasted Eggplant Caviar

Rye Caramelized Onion Dip

Black Olive Dip

Horseradish Cream Dip

Tarragon and Artichoke Dip

The Secret Guacamole

Roasted Carrot Hummus

Raw Spinach Dip

Aloo Gobi Dip

Middle Eastern Butternut Squash Purée

Edamame Dip

Deep in the midst of an Asian food phase, I was fascinated with edamame. I experimented with substituting the beans in every recipe I made for edamame. Clearly, I had some hits and some misses. One *hungry* evening at home, all I had in my fridge were frozen peas and frozen shelled edamame. Much like many New Yorkers, I also had a fridge full of condiments including ume plum, a Japanese plum that provides a fifth taste sensation described as umami. It isn't bitter, sweet, salty, or sour. It has a flavor that adds its own unique element to anything it's added to. The sweetness of the peas and the meatiness of the edamame are perfect partners, and combined with the ume plum . . . well, you have to taste it to believe it. I can eat this one with a spoon straight from the container, but it marries well with crudités, spread on crispy rice crackers or pita, served with tomato slices, or spooned on top of a pile of leafy steamed greens.

INGREDIENTS
$1/2$ bag frozen and shelled edamame

$1/2$ bag frozen sweet peas

1 Tbsp. ume plum paste (or a few splashes of ume plum vinegar)

1 Tbsp. nama shoyu (or a good soy sauce)

Crushed red pepper

Juice of one lime

1 cup good-quality olive oil

1–2 Tbsp. water

1. Throw the first six ingredients in a blender or a food processor. Slowly drizzle in the oil, adding more oil as needed. The mixture should be thick.

2. Thin with water, or add more oil depending on how you like your dip and what you intend as an end result.

3. Adjust seasoning as needed.

VARIATIONS

- $1/2$ tsp. dry powdered wasabi for a spicy kick.

- 1 Tbsp. raw tahini gives it a more savory and creamy taste.

- Handful of whole edamame or peas for more texture.

Roasted Garlic and Tomato Spread

This dip-cum-spread should come with the warning, "highly addictive." My friend Mike, genius chef and healer, was the inspiration for this recipe, as he taught me his technique of roasting garlic. We used to teach cooking classes together and he reminded me what a timesaver it is to roast whole heads of garlic and keep them in the fridge to use later.

You will want to make a good quantity of this dip, as it is very useful to have on hand. Feel free to eliminate the tomatoes and just use the garlic as a spread or add to any sauce or soup. Substituting peppers, onions, zucchini, or any other veggie in the sauce in place of the tomatoes is also a scrumptious option.

INGREDIENTS

2–3 heads of garlic, whole

One box grape, plum, or any small tomatoes

Olive oil

Salt to taste

1. Rub the garlic head with olive oil, wrap tightly in foil, and toss in the oven (the baseball technique of roasting, described in Chapter Six). Cook for about an hour or until soft to the touch.

2. Toss the tomatoes in a bit of olive oil, place on a cookie sheet, and pop in the oven for about 30 to 45 minutes. They will break down and get juicy.

3. Take the garlic out, slice the top off like a hat and squeeze out every last bit!

4. Mix with the tomatoes and season with salt, pepper, and crushed red pepper.

VARIATIONS

- Try serving this as a dip.
- Use instead of butter or olive oil for bread.
- Use as a sauce for rice noodles or pasta.

Roasted Eggplant Caviar

My friend Suz and I were in Greece—young and traveling on the cheap. We stayed only in small B&Bs, which were essentially rooms in someone's home. In order for us to get to our room, we had to pass through the owner's kitchen. The mama of the house, who spoke absolutely no English and rarely smiled, was always in the kitchen concocting some heavenly smelling brew. Each day I tried to see what vegetables or spices she was using or how she was using them, but every day she shooed me out of the kitchen with her broom. On our last day she gave in and let us taste her eggplant caviar. The roasted flavor of the eggplant combined with the spice blend she chose almost brought me to tears. It warmed my insides, and you could practically taste the love it was made with. Thank you for the inspiration, Greek Mama!

INGREDIENTS

1 large eggplant—about 2 lbs.

2 Tbsp. green olive oil

2 cloves of garlic, crushed

6 shallots, peeled and diced

Dash of cayenne pepper

3 Tbsp. lemon juice

$1/4$ cup fresh Italian parsley, chopped

1 Tbsp. mustard seeds, toasted

1. Slice the eggplant in half and put on a cookie sheet with the skin side down and broil for about 5 minutes.

2. Scoop out the pulp and let cool for a few minutes.

3. Put the oil, garlic, shallots, and pepper into a pan and cook for 5 minutes until they start to smell fragrant.

4. Put everything into a blender with the lemon juice, parsley, and the eggplant pulp and blend until smooth.

5. Serve at room temperature.

Rye Caramelized Onion Dip

Roy's NY, a Pan-Asian restaurant in downtown Manhattan, was the first restaurant I ever cooked at and was one of my all-time favorite jobs. I learned more about cooking on that line from the chef, Troy Guard, and from the other line cooks than I did in cooking school. Our open-kitchen had a wood-burning pizza oven in the front of the restaurant. That was my spot because Troy thought having a pretty girl up front sold more pizzas. My station was next to Bill the appetizer guy, who had the busiest post in the kitchen. It was part of my job to back him up. He yelled a lot, but he also taught me many useful tricks for which I am forever grateful. One of these was how to caramelize onions properly. He said, "Krulak—get your hands off the onions and leave them alone." The longer you let them cook, the sweeter and creamier they get. This dip is essentially nothing more than that. Slice them up and let them simmer . . .

INGREDIENTS

3 large red onions, sliced

3 large Spanish onions
(or any sweet, white onion will do)

Handful of caraway seeds

Pinch of hot red pepper or paprika

1 tsp. Dijon mustard
(or less, depending on taste; I like it strong)

1 tsp. cumin powder

Salt and pepper to taste

Olive oil as needed

1. Slice the onions and set aside.

2. Heat a large skillet and toast the caraway seeds until you hear a "pop" (about 30 seconds). Remove them immediately to a plate and let cool.

3. Toss the onions into the skillet with some oil and lower the flame. Let the onions start to soften, then add caraway, red pepper, Dijon mustard, and cumin powder.

4. Stir occasionally and let them cook for at least 20 minutes—the longer the better.

5. Season with salt and black pepper, and add a sprinkle of olive oil.

6. Serve as a dip or put in the blender with some more olive oil and use as a sauce or a dressing. This can sit in the fridge for up to one week in a glass jar.

VARIATIONS

* You can vary the types of onions for a deeper flavor.

* Use shallots, scallions, even leeks. The spices can vary as well.

* Eliminate Dijon or try toasted mustard seeds, a pinch of cinnamon, or even some garam masala.

Black Olive Dip

Italians make purées sold in small jars to use as starters for sauces, or sometimes a tablespoon of the purée with a bit of olive oil is actually the sauce itself. I discovered these purées when I was staying in Rome and ended up carrying back an entire suitcase full of every type imaginable. I don't even want to think of how many Euros I spent on puréed vegetables in jars. I grew especially fond of the black olive purée and tried a dab on almost anything I was eating to see what it went best with. I carried a little jar around in my bag to try it on pizza, vegetables, or just to nibble on with crudités. The restaurant owners often gave me odd looks, but I got used to that in Italy. Seems that I was always doing something or eating something that wasn't quite acceptable to the Romans.

INGREDIENTS

1 cup assorted black olives, pitted
(green are delicious as well)

1/2 cup high-quality olive oil

1/2 tsp. good salt

1 clove garlic (optional)

1. Put the olives, salt, and garlic in a blender on low or mini Cuisinart and start the motor.
2. Slowly drizzle in the oil, increasing the speed.

FASCINATING FACT

Olives are almost like baby avocados; rich in good fats that our bodies need.

Horseradish Cream Dip

From inspiration I received on a recent trip to Israel, this recipe evolved from passable to exceptional. While wandering around the Ha Carmel market in Tel Aviv, I saw some horse-radish that a vendor had displayed on a table near his stall. I have a high heat threshold, so I didn't hesitate to try it. The man must have known that I was going to have a shock, as he handed me some apple to cool my palate. Not only did this work quickly, but I had an ah-ha moment about the horse-radish dip! The perfect partner for the root and the key to unlocking its round bitterness is apple! I am so grateful to that horseradish vendor not only for clearing my sinuses, but for teaching me new palate-cooling tricks.

This is heavenly as a dip for roasted beet fries or on top of any grilled vegetable or even a burger.

> Note: Shredded horseradish is very strong and will open your sinuses in much the same crisp way that wasabi does.

INGREDIENTS

1 4" piece of horseradish root,
skinned and cut into big chunks

3/4 cup olive oil

1/4 cup apple cider vinegar

1/4 apple, shredded

1 tsp. anise (fennel) seeds

1. Shred the root and the apple and set aside.

2. Add the olive oil, vinegar, and apple.

3. Mix in a bowl or a blender and thin with water if desired.

4. Add salt and pepper to taste.

Tarragon and Artichoke Dip

One cold New York winter, I swapped my Chelsea apartment with a girl in Rome. Her flat was located next to the famous Campo de Fiori, the large square in the center of Rome that has one of the grandest and most colorful open-air markets in Rome. By day, the Campo is brimming with some of the most stunning fruits, vegetables, and flowers I have ever seen in my life. The air is always filled with the fragrance of freshly baked breads and pizzas from the "forno (the ovens) di Campo de Fiori." The square is lined with outdoor cafés and bars, so at night it is full of people and always a scene. It is truly an extraordinary spot and feels very "Roman." Just off one of the side streets is a little restaurant/market called Roscioli's. I was staying just around the corner, so I frequented the market/wine shop/restaurant—a lot. I must have spent a month's rent on their sublime, grilled artichokes. They wouldn't tell me how they made them, but at twenty Euros a kilo, they must have been made with gold. Organic grilled artichokes in jars are easy to find in specialty shops and in most large supermarkets. They are not exactly the same as Roscioli's, but not a bad compromise without flying back to Rome. Which is not a bad option either . . .

INGREDIENTS

4–5 fresh or grilled artichokes kept in oil

Handful of fresh tarragon (or 2 Tbsp. dried tarragon)

Salt and pepper to taste

1. Roughly chop the fresh tarragon and set aside in a wet paper towel.
2. Roughly chop the artichokes and mix the tarragon.
3. Mix together and serve on toast or as a dip for crudités.

A CARNIVORE'S CHOICE

This recipe is excellent mixed with high-quality Italian tuna.

The Secret Guacamole

My brothers don't compliment my cooking very often. For my brother Rob to look up and say, "This is the best guacamole I have ever had!" is extraordinarily high praise. This is lighter than most guacamoles and moves through the body easily because of its high cellulose content. In simpler terms, it has celery in it.

I am passionate for avocados and prefer to use crudités to scoop them out of the shell. Somehow, the crudités ended up in the mix. The celery adds its natural salt and, combined with the lime, adds a depth and a spark to the avocado that is really spectacular. In addition, the celery helps break down the natural fat in the avocado so you won't feel as "full," which can sometimes happen when eating a pile of avocados.

INGREDIENTS

3 medium avocados

4 stalks of celery, chopped

1 small bunch of cilantro, roughly chopped

1 or 2 limes, juiced

1 tsp. maple syrup

1 medium red bell pepper, finely diced

1 jalapeno pepper, seeds discarded
and finely diced

Splash of nama shoyu or soy sauce

Big pinch of crushed red pepper

Salt to taste

1. Mash the jalapeno and the red pepper in a mortar and pestle or in the bottom of a bowl with the lime juice.

2. Cut the avocados in half and squeeze out into the bowl with the mash, mixing well with the lime juice. Keep at least one or two of the pits in the bowl while mixing to keep the gorgeous vibrant green color.

3. Mix all of the other ingredients in, taste for seasoning.

4. You may need some more lime juice and more salt or even a dash more of the nama shoyu to bring out more of the flavor.

5. Serve with crudité or homemade baked tortilla chips.

Roasted Carrot Hummus

There are moments in our lives that are like little snapshots we wish we could keep in a book. My time in Delhi was most certainly one of them. One New Year's Eve my friend Sarah and her ever-so-charming husband, Vishal, hosted a long weekend in the countryside north of New Delhi. It was a long weekend in a haveli (similar to a chateau) with nothing much to do but eat, drink, and enjoy one another's company. It was a motley crew of guests—an artist couple, Vishal's aunt and uncle, my mother and me, and a few others who popped in and out. We were all wrapped up in blankets and crouched around portable heaters, as it was winter and winters in northern India are moist. In a house like the one we were in, with stone walls and cement floors, there was no retained heat. Since the kitchen was the warmest place in the house, I cooked a lot that weekend.

INGREDIENTS

1 lb. carrots, roughly chopped

$1/2$ small red onion, roughly chopped

2 cloves garlic (if you have leftover roasted garlic, it's perfect here)

$1/2$ tsp. cumin (or more to taste)

$1/8$–$1/4$ cup tahini (I prefer a raw tahini)

About $1/2$ cup olive oil
(less or more depending on thickness desired)

Salt to taste

Coriander and sesame seeds for topping

1. Process the carrots, onion, garlic, and tahini in a food processor and drizzle in the olive oil.

2. Add the spices to taste.

3. Top with chopped coriander and sesame seeds.

VARIATION

This recipe is excellent when made with roasted carrots or flash-boiled carrots. For roasted carrots, use the recipe in the "small plates" section for roasting vegetables and roast the carrots and onions together for about 35 minutes.

Raw Spinach Dip

Dark leafy greens are hard to come by in France. Now and then you can find a tall bunch of chard, rainbow chard, or a random bunch of something that resembles kale, but isn't really kale. These greens can usually only be found at organic markets, and often one must request them. They frequently sell out early. As my diet is heavy on the dark leafy greens and light on the animal proteins, France was a challenge at times. Spinach can be found at most markets. One Sunday morning at the Le Marché Boulevard Raspail (an organic open-air market in Paris), the famous French actress, Juliette Binoche, was hoarding the spinach and I tried to nudge her out of the way before I noticed who she was. After recognizing her, I backed off. I am a big fan, after all.

This dip was pantry happenstance—meaning it was made with whatever was around and it tasted heavenly. Switch the parsley with cilantro or any green herb you have for variety.

INGREDIENTS

1 bunch organic spinach

1 bunch parsley

$1/2$ cup olive oil

1 clove garlic, smashed

Juice of 1 lemon

1 Tbsp. tahini

Salt to taste

1. Mash the garlic and the tahini in a bowl with the lemon juice.

2. Put all ingredients in a food processor or a blender and blend until smooth.

Aloo Gobi Dip

Two dear American expat friends of mine were living in Delhi during the same time I was. I had the good fortune of living at their house for a while. Vinay worked for the U.S. government and they lived in a beautiful house in one of the most prestigious sections of New Delhi, complete with a backyard, American appliances, and full staff. Kishan, the cook, only cooked Indian foods. We tried to teach him some American options, but he was much more comfortable with his spice box and his dhal or lentils. Kishan's spice combinations were extraordinary and his food tasted light as opposed to much Indian food, which can leave you feeling full and heavy. Home-cooked Indian food is very different from any that one would taste in a restaurant.

I actually won't eat at Indian restaurants anymore because of this! This dip is a twist on one of Kishan's dishes—the spice combo, purely Kishan; the ratio of veg to starch, all mine.

INGREDIENTS

1 cauliflower

$^1/_2$ jicama, sliced

$^1/_2$–1 cup olive oil
(depending on preferred thickness of dip)

1 tsp. cumin

2 cloves garlic

Organic butter or coconut oil
for greasing pan

Salt to taste

Small handful of coriander leaves,
chopped for garnish

1. Cut cauliflower into small florets.

2. Toss with olive oil, cumin, salt, and whole garlic cloves.

3. Oil a cookie sheet with butter or coconut oil and place the cauliflower on the sheet.

4. Roast the cauliflower on 375 for about 30 minutes.

5. When the cauliflower is finished cooking, remove from the oven and let cool slightly.

6. Place the cauliflower in a blender (or food processor) with the jicama and begin to blend, adding the olive oil slowly. The desired thickness of the dip will determine the amount of oil added.

7. Adjust the seasoning to taste. I normally add more cumin and salt at this point.

8. Serve with fresh coriander.

Middle Eastern Butternut Squash Purée

Moments of brilliance happen from time to time. This dip was one of them. There is a Middle Eastern spice called Raz El Hanout that I was introduced to when I was in university in Paris. Raz El Hanout is a Moroccan spice that is used across Northern Africa, and as I was taught, every family or restaurant makes their own personal blend of the spice. Over the Jewish high holidays, I was invited to my friend Hana's parents' house for dinner. Hana's mother made a gorgeous feast of Sephardic Jewish delicacies. My background is 100% Ashkenazi, meaning my family is from Eastern Europe. The food I was brought up on was dramatically different from what I saw on my friend's holiday table. They had stews, crispy rice dishes, couscous, and tagine—dishes that I had never even seen before. This was my first introduction to Moroccan food, let alone Jewish Moroccan food, and the spices were surreal in my mouth. But I will never forget the one spice that stood out the most—Hana's mother said the dish was called "crispy rice," as the rice was burned on the bottom and then steamed on top, and the spice was added in after it was cooked. I kept tasting it over and over again, trying to figure out what was in the Raz El Hanout. Hana's grandmother came over to me, put her hand on my shoulder, and said that I never would.

INGREDIENTS

1 butternut squash, halved,
deseeded, peeled, and cubed

1 head garlic, roasted

1/4 cup olive oil

1/2 cup vegetable broth
(bouillon, boxed or freshly made)

1 tsp. (or more) Raz el Hanout

Salt to taste

1. Oil the garlic and wrap in foil; roast at 400 degrees for one hour.

2. Place the squash in a pot of boiling water for about 20 minutes or until tender.

3. Drain the squash in a colander and place in a blender with $1/4$ cup olive oil and the vegetable broth and blend on high.

4. Add the garlic and spice.

5. Blend and taste.

CHAPTER FOUR

Convertible Broth-Based Soups

These soothing, thick soups incorporate vegetable broth or bouillon and puréed vegetables. "Fixings" are integrated for flavor, color, and texture. This is why I call them "convertible," as they are mutable depending on your mood, taste, and desire. The soups can easily be used as sauces or dressings for other dishes such as roasted veggies, fish, pasta, or even quinoa.

As for preparation and equipment, a blender will yield a smoother soup that is more uniform in color and texture, as opposed to a food processor that leaves flakes or tiny surprises in the broth. For most of these soups, the starter base is the same. It is then altered by the vegetables and herbs used. I have used a vegetable broth or water, but chicken, beef, or fish broth would work brilliantly and create an entirely new soup flavor.

The Basic Formula

INGREDIENTS

Garlic	Water
Broth, stock, or bouillon	The vegetables
Onions, leeks, or scallions	The herbs and spices
Texture (add-ins and fixings)	

HOW TO CLEAN A LEEK

Dirt and stones are often caught inside the little green and white layers of a leek. The simplest method I've found to clean a leek is to chop off the dark green leaves and set aside. Cut the leek in half lengthwise. Chop the leek into 1" or 2" pieces and loosen the layers. Soak the pieces in a bowl of cold water for at least 5 minutes to let the stones fall to the bottom of the bowl. Drain and rinse well.

I like to use the dark green parts of the leek as well, and find that they have a nice flavor. The very top portion of the leek's leaves are tough and, unless cooked to death, next to impossible to eat. However, the middle portion has a delightful, mild flavor.

FASCINATING FACTS

Because thick soups are primarily blended vegetables or greens, they are filled with vitamins and other nutrients that move through the body with ease. Blended foods are essentially pre-digested foods, almost like baby foods, and are easier for the body to assimilate. The result is that your body receives the nutrient, given that you "chew" the soup a bit and don't just drink it in one gulp.

Recipes Included in This Chapter

The Basic Convertible Cooked Soup Starter

Gazpacho

Sweet Pea Soup with Hot Chili Oil

Roasted Carrot Ginger Soup

Broccoli Broth with Roasted Vegetables

Grilled Corn Chowder

Roasted Onion & Parsnip Soup with Curry and Hot Chili

Roasted Fennel Soup

Celery Root Soup

Smooth Jerusalem Artichoke Stew with Mushrooms and Greens

The Basic Convertible Cooked Soup Starter

This can be used as a starter guide for most of the convertible broth recipes. It also serves as your launch pad for creativity.

INGREDIENTS

1 Tbsp. olive oil

1 Tbsp. coconut oil (or organic butter)

2 red onions

2 white onions (or 2 leeks, well cleaned)

1 or 2 cloves garlic, peeled and smashed

3 cups vegetable broth (or any broth you choose)

2 cups water (or use all water or all broth)

1. Heat the olive oil and the coconut oil in a large pot.

2. Add the leeks or onions (or both) and the smashed garlic and cook for about five minutes, stirring frequently.

3. Add a pinch of salt.

4. Continue to cook until the leeks, onion, and garlic are soft and translucent. (If they begin to brown too much on the bottom as they cook, add a splash of the veggie broth.)

5. From here you will add your main ingredients, such as roasted vegetables, cooked vegetables, or pretty much any vegetable you can get your hands on.

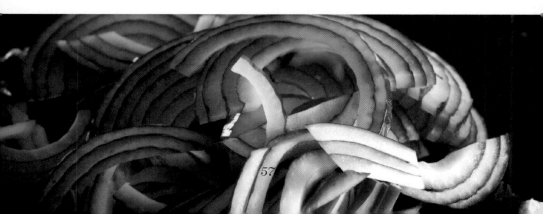

Gazpacho

The summer before I went to University in Paris I did the "10 countries in two weeks" with a Euro-pass, a small bag, and a college friend. We stayed in a few hostels, sat at many a café, met many a boy, had a few fights, and went to a few museums. By the time we reached Barcelona we wanted nothing to do with one another. I decided it was time to see some culture and ventured out on my own. On my way out of the hotel I met some boys from Torino, Italy, whom we had seen on the train. They had a full day of sightseeing planned, starting with a tour of the Gaudi buildings and followed by the Picasso Museum. They invited me to join them, and who was I to refuse four adorable Italians? We passed a gorgeous day in Barcelona, laughed a lot, and ended up near the water for a very late lunch of gazpacho, tortilla, and sangria. The way the soup was served left such an impression on me that I will never forget it. Each ingredient was served separately so I could choose what and how much I wanted in my soup. This was the best gazpacho I had ever eaten, but of course when a 19-year-old girl from Cleveland is sitting seaside with four hot Italian men, what wouldn't be good?

INGREDIENTS

$1/4$ cup sun-dried tomatoes, soaked in water until soft
(just enough to cover the tomatoes)

2 cups tomatoes crudely cut
(I like to use the most fragrant tomatoes,
which are usually Roma, heirloom, or oversized cherry)

1 Tbsp. garlic, diced

$1/2$ cup fresh basil, roughly chopped

1 Tbsp. dried oregano

1 English cucumber, peeled and chopped

2 scallions, chopped

Pinch of cinnamon

Dash of balsamic vinegar

1. Blend ³/₄ of the ingredients and pulse until well blended but not smooth—small chunks of vegetables should remain.

2. Use the remaining ¹/₄ ingredients to stir in the soup to add chunkiness. Optionally, you can leave them out and let your guests choose which ingredients to add.

3. Delicious when topped with chopped black olives and crushed red chili pepper.

Sweet Pea Soup with Hot Chili Oil

I hold this soup dear in my heart, as it is the first soup I ever made for a date. I saw Ming Tsai make a similar one on his PBS show back in the 90s and was inspired by its simplicity and bright green, healthful color. I have always loved a warm bowl of pea soup with crunchy croutons, but was never a fan of the bacon or the color. The green peas lighten up the classic soup while adding a subtle sweetness; the spinach adds both color and extra nutrients in the rawest, healthiest form.

INGREDIENTS

2 roughly chopped red onions

2 smashed garlic cloves

4-ish cups veggie stock—preferably homemade,
but organic boxed works well
(I have used a bouillon for this soup in a pinch
and it worked out well)

2 cups (or 1 bag) organic, frozen sweet peas

1 bag pre-washed organic spinach

1 Tbsp. olive oil

1 Tbsp. butter (or coconut oil)

1. Heat the olive oil and butter or coconut oil in a large sauce-pan and throw the roughly chopped onions and the smashed garlic in to soften and make sure not to brown them. This is a process called "sweating."

2. Add stock, salt, and pepper and bring to a boil. Make sure the broth is leaning toward the salty side. It will mellow when the peas and the spinach are added.

3. When the stock is boiling, add peas and cook until soft. This will be about 5-ish minutes.

4. Turn off the flame and add the whole bag of spinach (it's a little trick to give the soup a beautiful bright green color).

5. Immediately purée the soup with a hand blender or put into blender or Vitamix®. Check for seasoning.

CHILI OIL

There are several bottled chili oils available, but a fresh one is quite simple to make.

INGREDIENTS

$1/2$ cup olive oil

1 Tbsp. chili powder (or cayenne pepper)

$1/4$ tsp. cumin

2 scallions, sliced to sprinkle on top of the soup
(I like to use both the dark and light green parts.)

1. Quickly toast the spices in a moderately hot, dry sauté pan and take off the flame. You will know they are cooked when you start to smell the spices. It's under a minute.

2. Pour the olive oil over the spices in a mason jar or any glass jar with a lid and let sit overnight. It will separate, but shake it up before you drizzle it on top of the soup.

3. To serve, ladle the bright green soup in a bowl or mug and drizzle about $1/2$ tsp. of the oil on top and sprinkle some sliced scallions on top.

FASCINATING FACT

Spinach is added last in the soup preparation to keep the color bright green and to add extra nutrients.

A CARNIVORE'S CHOICE

This is delicious with crispy salmon skin sprinkled on top or organic Bresaola, which is an air-dried salted beef. You may even try turkey bacon or a "facon" as traditional pea soup has bacon in it. I also like it with crumbled goat or feta cheese.

Roasted Carrot Ginger Soup

In the Northern Indian town of Rishikesh there is a little dhaba, which is the Indian version of a coffee shop, called Mukti's. Each day after yoga class at the Omkarananda Ashram, my friends Ravi, Mike, and I had lunch there. Mukti's had six tables, two cooktop burners, six pots, and a big fire pit out back that he shared with a few other dhabas on the block. I don't remember ever seeing a refrigerator, which meant that the produce was bought fresh each day. His was some of the best Indian food I have ever eaten. Mukti's masterpieces were twists on traditional Indian classics. As Rishikesh is a popular destination for Israelis, Middle Eastern spices turned up in much of the food. Mukti was happy to let me watch him cook—he had no choice, as there was only one room. I was surprised at how he melted ghee (clarified butter) with fresh tahini to use as a base for stir-fried vegetables or soup. This soup is his recipe almost verbatim. Why mess with perfection? I did replace the ghee with coconut oil.

INGREDIENTS

2 Tbsp. coconut oil (or ghee)

1 Tbsp. tahini

2 red onions, sliced

2 cloves garlic, smashed

3 cups vegetable broth (or water plus bouillon cube)

1 1/2 pound carrots, roughly chopped

2 Tbsp. ginger, grated with the juice reserved.

1 tsp. coriander powder

1 tsp. cumin

1 tsp. cinnamon

2 tsp. fresh lime juice

Pinch of hot red pepper

3 Tbsp. fresh cilantro, chopped

1. Preheat the oven to 400 degrees F.

2. Divide the carrots into 3 or 4 piles and wrap each pile tightly in foil.

3. Place the carrots on a cookie sheet in the oven and roast for at least 30 to 45 minutes. Check the bundles after 30 minutes to see how they are cooking. They should be softening and smelling sweet.

4. Toast the cumin and coriander in the bottom of a large hot soup pot for about 20 seconds to release the oils and the flavor. Remove and set aside.

5. Heat the coconut oil and the tahini in the same large pot.

6. Add the onions and the smashed garlic and cook for about five minutes, stirring frequently, until the onion and garlic are soft and translucent. If the pot begins to brown too much on the bottom as they cook, add a bit of the veggie broth. You do not want them to brown. Add the salt. You will want to adjust this at the end as well.

7. Add the roasted carrots and the ginger to the pot and let meld with the other ingredients.

8. Add the broth or water or both and season with salt and pepper and cinnamon.

9. Ladle into big bowls and top with fresh cilantro.

Broccoli Broth with Roasted Vegetables

I honestly don't even know where this soup recipe came from, but I do know that I missed broccoli when I was in Asia. Cauliflower is popular, while broccoli is more of a western thing. I am guessing this came about when I was in a "purée-anything" phase. The broth is creamy and luscious, lending itself easily to additional toppings or fixings. I have often put the soup on top of fish or quinoa.

It has become a staple in my home and many of my friends and clients' homes. After you make it and serve it once, I promise it will become a staple in yours as well. This lasts at least four days in the fridge and up to two weeks in the freezer. I also like to freeze it in cubes to have as a snack or melt into other soups.

INGREDIENTS

1 or 2 large heads of broccoli

$1/2$ to 1 bag spinach

Salt (the water needs to be salty as this is your "broth")

4 to 5 cups water

$1/2$ cup olive oil, plus a bit more to drizzle on top for finishing

Handful of chopped olives
(I prefer black as I love the taste and they look nicer.)

1. Bring a large potful of very salty water to a rapid boil.

2. Cut the florets off the head of the broccoli and put in the water.

3. Cover and let cook for about 4 to 5 minutes—the broccoli should be tender, but not too soft.

4. Drain broccoli but reserve the cooking water.

5. Place broccoli florets in a blender with about $1/4$ of the cooking water and purée until smooth and to desired thickness. Add spinach and blend.

6. (Optional step) If you would like to add olive oil to the broth, now is the time. Blend in about $^1/_4$–$^1/_2$ cup olive oil.

7. Pour into bowls and season to taste with salt and a pinch of crushed red pepper (optional), a drizzle of olive oil, and a sprinkling of black olives.

VARIATIONS

- Top with crumbled feta or goat cheese.
- Sprinkle with Parmesan cheese.
- Add crunchy croutons.
- Use chunky steamed or roasted vegetables.
- Add a dash of chili oil.
- Swirl this soup with another soup—perhaps the Parsnip or the Corn soup.
- Pour the soup over rice noodles, rice, or quinoa for a heartier meal.

Grilled Corn Chowder

While traveling in southern India I once saw a man on the side of the road grilling corn on the cob. Our driver stopped to get a piece, as he said it was his favorite. I wasn't so into eating corn grilled on a little roadside fire by a squatting man in Northern India. I had no idea how old the corn was or where it came from, and there were no cornfields in sight. It made me grow nostalgic for New York summer corn that is both abundant and sweet. I bought some from the man by the road and took it home. The corn was chewy, overcooked, and impossible to eat off the cob. I cut it off the cob and threw it in a blender with broth and olive oil. With a bit more tweaking, this soup was the result.

INGREDIENTS

3 cups fresh corn cut off the cob
(grilled, roasted, or raw)

Reserve $1/2$ cup or so of the corn
to add chunkiness to the soup

Celtic Sea Salt® to taste

1 clove garlic, diced

Fresh pepper to taste

1 Tbsp. fresh rosemary, chopped

1 Tbsp. fresh sage, chopped

2 cups water or vegetable broth

$1/4$ cup red bell pepper, diced (for garnish)

1. In a medium saucepan, heat the water or broth and bring to a simmer.

2. Add the corn, garlic, and the herbs and bring to a boil.

3. Turn down the heat and let simmer for 10 minutes.

4. Season with salt and pepper to taste.

5. Purée the soup.

6. To serve, ladle into bowls, sprinkle with some of the reserved corn kernels and some chopped red bell pepper.

VARIATIONS

- Eliminate the rosemary and sage and add a handful of chopped cilantro at the end.

- Grilling, roasting, or leaving the corn raw is really your choice. Corn in its season is heavenly when raw as it is at its sweetest.

- To roast or grill, place the whole shucked cob on the grill or in the oven at 400 degrees for about 5–7 minutes, turning occasionally.

Roasted Onion & Parsnip Soup with Curry and Hot Chili

My mother used to take my brothers and me to a restaurant in Cleveland called the Cheese Cellar for French onion soup. From what I remember, every dish in the restaurant was topped with Gruyère cheese. I can still taste the salty/sweet, chewy, deep, rich flavor of the soup and hear the crunch of the crisp, toasty bread served alongside for dipping. My brother Rob and I were recently having a nostalgic moment for the soup, but since I no longer eat cow cheese, beef broth, or white bread, I was left wondering how to reproduce this flavor. Although this is very different from the French onion soup of our childhood, the rich roasted onions and parsnip somehow mimic the deep beef broth flavor that sets the tone for an old world French onion soup.

INGREDIENTS

1 pound red and white onions, roughly chopped

$1/_2$ pound parsnips, roughly chopped

3–4 cups vegetable broth

1 Tbsp. curry powder

$1/_2$ Tbsp. chili powder

2 Tbsp. olive oil

2 Tbsp. coconut oil

Salt and pepper to taste

1. Preheat the oven to 400 degrees F.

2. Toss the onions, parsnips, olive oil, coconut oil, and curry powder into a Dutch oven or roasting pan and place in the oven for about 40 minutes or until soft, stirring occasionally.

3. Remove the pot from the oven and place on the stove over medium heat.

4. Add the broth and chili powder. Let the soup cook for at least 20 minutes.

5. Season with salt and pepper to taste.

6. The soup should be thick and creamy.

7. Top with cheese, chopped parsley, arugula or spinach.

Roasted Fennel Soup

INGREDIENTS

2 red onions

2 yellow onions

2 shallots, chopped

3–4 cups diced fennel
(Reserve the arms and fronds
for garnish and dressings)

1 Tbsp. fennel seeds, crushed

4 cups veggie stock

$1/_2$ tsp. chopped thyme

1. Heat some olive oil in a large saucepan and throw the roughly chopped onions and the smashed garlic in to sweat and soften (do not brown them).

2. Add stock, salt, and pepper and bring to a boil. Make sure the broth is leaning toward the salty side—it will mellow out when the peas and the spinach are added.

3. When the stock is boiling, add peas and cook until soft. This will be about 5-ish minutes.

4. Turn off the flame and add the whole bag of spinach (again, it's a little trick to give the soup a beautiful bright green color).

5. Immediately purée the soup in the blender.

6. Taste-test for seasoning.

Celery Root Soup

Celery root is a very French vegetable. There was nothing similar in Cleveland while I was growing up, but I was 19 years old, living in Paris, and ready to absorb the culture. My new friend Lisa, a very tall and beautiful model from a hippy family in Vancouver, Canada, had been introducing me to the world of vegetarianism, health food shops, and the art of dry skin brushing. She had already been living in Paris for four years and knew the ins and outs of the fresh markets—how to shop at them and which stalls to go to. Lisa could spot a ripe vegetable and discard an improperly grown one better than the market men themselves. She was so strikingly beautiful that they were happy to let her pick through the vegetables to show me her tricks. I grew up in the suburbs with Iggy the Fruit Man delivering our fruits and veggies weekly, and we never really had any choice. For me, this was like Disneyland! From our market shopping, Lisa taught me about French winter soups and the vegetables that were used most often. I had never had a celery root or a leek, but I instantly fell in love with the rich, deep, almost sweet flavor of the soup. Her soup was chunky, finished with cream, and a pinch of nutmeg. This is my rendition without the cream, but still creamy enough to warm your bones during the cold, rainy days of a Parisian winter.

INGREDIENTS

1 Tbsp. olive oil

1 Tbsp. coconut oil or organic butter

1 leek, cleaned and chopped

1 large sweet white onion, chopped

2 garlic cloves, peeled

One large celery root (about 3 pounds), peeled and cut into rough cubes

3 cups vegetable stock

3 cups water (or can use all water and no vegetable stock, if you like)

Salt and white pepper to taste

A pinch of hot chili powder

1. Heat the olive oil and the coconut oil in a large pot.

2. Add the leek and onion and cook for about five minutes, stirring frequently. Add the garlic cloves and a pinch of salt.

3. Continue to cook until the leeks, onion, and garlic are soft and translucent. If they begin to brown too much on the bottom as they cook, add a bit of the veggie broth.

4. Toss in the celery root and add the stock (or use all water).

5. Bring to a boil, then reduce to a strong simmer. Cook with the pot lid on top, but slightly off-kilter, letting the celery root pieces soften. This should take about 45 minutes.

6. Season with the white pepper and chili powder

7. Purée the soup in the blender until smooth. If the soup is too thick, it can be thinned with water or stock.

8. Taste, and season with additional salt and pepper if desired.

VARIATIONS

- Finish with a pinch of nutmeg.
- Add mushrooms.
- Top with shaved truffles.
- Swirl with another soup.
- Or, of course, top with chopped black olives.

Smooth Jerusalem Artichoke Stew with Mushrooms and Greens

My cousin Karen grows the most abundant amount of sunchokes (a.k.a. Jerusalem artichokes) I have ever seen. I picked about six pounds of sunchokes a few summers ago; however, I didn't know what to do with them, so I figured soup would be the best solution. Jerusalem artichokes are a remarkably alkalizing vegetable with high fiber content. They contain inulin, which breaks down fructose. In other words, sunchokes are a non-starchy carbohydrate that aids in digestion. The chokes hide dirt in the nooks and crannies, so I recommend soaking and even spraying them with a kitchen sink sprayer until they are clean.

The recipe below was the result of pure experimentation. It was one of those rare moments when I said out loud to myself, "Damn, you are good."

FASCINATING FACT

Jerusalem artichokes do not come from Jerusalem, nor do they look anything like artichokes. They are a member of the sunflower family, and the edible part is the tuber.

INGREDIENTS

1 pound Jerusalem artichokes, scrubbed

$1/2$ pound kale (or other dark leafy green), roughly chopped

Large handful of mushrooms, sliced (I like to use oyster or a mixture of wild mushrooms), roughly chopped

1. Toss the chokes into a giant stockpot and let them cook and soften in a small amount of water until they get smooth and creamy. This takes about an hour. Keep checking the chokes and stir occasionally. Add the mushrooms about half way through.

2. Add the greens and let it cook until greens soften.

CHAPTER FIVE

Blended and Crunchy Raw Salads

Fresh salads and greens are the main staple food in my diet—so much so that my friends have nicknamed me "leafy," "salad girl," "veggie goddess," and those are only a few. I answer to all of them with pride. Salads are often thought of as meal starters, or perhaps they bring back a memory of a wedge of iceberg lettuce topped with Hellmann's mayo, as my grandfather loved. Much more than that, they can be hearty main courses or a beautiful addition to any menu. I began exploring and experimenting with the main course salad each time I returned from India, where it was difficult to get a simple bowl of greens, but easy to get a big bowl of raw, chopped cabbage.

Salads in *Veggies for Carnivores* are divided into two main categories: Blended Salads and Crunchy Salads. A blended salad is a puréed combination of raw salad ingredients. Often called a green smoothie or a raw soup, it is essentially a salad in the blender. This luscious smooth and creamy salad base is the starting point for the addition of texture or "fixings."

A crunchy salad is one in which all of the ingredients, excluding the greens, are shredded, chopped, or sliced and added on top of the greens as "fixings."

There are a few important and classic techniques for cutting and preparing the different types of salad ingredients. Much like different varieties of pasta, each technique in chopping or shredding, for example, yields a different result for the vegetable. The way it feels in the mouth, the way it will hold sauce or dressing, the way it blends with the other ingredients—each of these details creates variation of flavor and texture. As a rule of thumb, I encourage people to veer toward the most seasonal, organic, local ingredients because they are both healthier and tastier than conventional or imported ingredients.

Recipes Included in This Chapter

The Basic Blended Salad

Basic Shredded Salad

Shredded Beet, Jicama, and Cabbage Slaw

Shredded Green Stuff Salad

Basic Chopped Salad

The Swirly Salad

Salad 101

The Basic Blended Salad

I would love to take full credit for conceptualizing blending raw vegetables, but this idea predates me. Ann Wigmore, the mother of the raw food movement, originated her recipes for blending sprouts and vegetables into smoothies during the early 1960s.

The blended salad has revolutionized many of my clients' lives as well as helped to whittle pounds off their waistlines. Some have re-grown hair; most have improved skin tone and eyesight, as well as increased energy. These drinks are an exceptional way to "eat" your greens while the enzymes inside them remain alive and intact. Think of the Blended Salad as a vegetable smoothie—it is much like the fruit smoothie, only made with vegetables.

The Formula

$1/_2$ to whole avocado

A large handful of greens
(Romaine lettuce plus another dark green
vegetable such as arugula, spinach,
or kale, or all of them.)

$1/_2$ pear

$1/_2$ lime, lemon, or orange
(or a combination of the 3)—juiced

1. Scoop out the avocado and put into the blender.

2. Put all of the remaining ingredients in the blender with enough water to cover, about 1 cup. I like my smoothies thick, but the amount of water varies depending on how much avocado and greens are used.

3. If you would like to use more pear or substitute with apple, this is also a neutral fruit and will produce a similar result.

VARIATIONS

Optional items to add flavor to the blended salad:

- Tomatoes
- Fennel
- Dandelion greens
- Red or yellow pepper

- Banana
- Coconut
- Coconut water
- Pineapple

For toppings or fixings:

- Chopped olives
- Chopped peppers
- Shredded nori or dulse (edible seaweed)

- Chopped celery
- Chopped fennel

Be creative!

Basic Shredded Salad

Shredding vegetables is a very common preparation in India. At first annoyed that my vegetables were seemingly dismantled and demoted to garnishes, I quickly grew to love the little piles of shredded cabbage or carrots served alongside every dish. As with most Indian cuisine, the way it is prepared often has to do with how it is digested. This goes even as far as the spice combinations, which are strategic in Indian cuisine. But in the case of shredding, the rationale is that if a food is blended or cut into smaller pieces, it is easier to chew and, ultimately, easier to digest. When eaten alongside a heavier meal, the shredded veggies will ease digestion.

The shredding technique lends itself to enormous creativity by mixing and matching colors, vegetable varieties, and even leaves. I'll often shred an assortment of vegetables, leave them to marinate for several hours, and then toss the mixture on top of lettuce just before serving.

SHREDDING TECHNIQUES

MANDOLINE

A mandoline delivers a fine and uniform cut and helps speed up the chopping process. However, a mandoline comes with a warning. **Use the plastic hand protector or a towel.** Microplane® also makes a protector glove that works brilliantly. As I have previously mentioned, I have *mandolined* the tops of my fingers more times than I care to remember and it hurts. Fingertips may grow back, but I don't advise testing my theory.

I have provided a list of my favorite brands in the front of the book. It is not necessary to spend a great deal of money to buy a good one. The Japanese-made mandolines are fantastic and only cost about $20.

A SHARP KNIFE

A very sharp knife is always useful for shredding a salad. I keep a chantry knife sharpener around, as I do not like to use a stone and find that if one does not know how to use a sharpening stone properly, it can actually make your knives duller.

Shredded Beet, Jicama, and Cabbage Slaw

While living in Southern India, my friends and I would often host potluck dinner parties. Without a doubt, several versions of a shredded salad would be brought to the table. Because root vegetables and cabbage are pretty much the only vegetables that are grown year round in Southern India due to the difficult growing seasons and monsoon seasons, the salads would inevitably be made of carrots, beets, an Indian gourd, and perhaps some cabbage.

Inspired by my friends, this slaw and all of the various combinations and dressings are made with ingredients that can be found anywhere in the world—minus the jicama, which could easily be replaced by daikon radish, parsnip, white carrot, or simply left out. The jicama is sweet and a parsnip would be as well, whereas a daikon would be more neutral in flavor.

I recommend using the carrot dressing with this slaw, but it is delicious with any of the dressings and sauces.

INGREDIENTS

$1/2$ head small red cabbage,
sliced thin (shredded)

$1/2$ head small Napa cabbage,
sliced thin (shredded)

2 small beets, shredded

1 large jicama, shredded

3 Tbsp. currants, soaked (or raisins)

2 Tbsp. black sesame seeds (white are fine as well)

1. Toss all of the ingredients together with dressings but reserve $1/2$ tsp. of the sesame seeds to top the salad before serving.

2. Let marinate for at least 30 minutes before serving. This gets better as it sits.

Shredded Green Stuff Salad

This monochromatic salad has absolutely no story except that I liked the idea of a shredded salad that was all one color. It is important to keep the lettuce separate from the marinating vegetables until serving or the lettuce will get soggy.

INGREDIENTS

1 medium cucumber

1 fennel

1 zucchini

1 bunch of kale cut in shreds

2 large handfuls of mache or any dark, small leaf such as arugula

$^1/_2$ head butter lettuce, ripped into shreds

1cup frozen sweet peas, thawed

Sunflower sprouts (or sprouts of your choice)

Dressing or sauce of choice from Chapter Two

1. Shred the cucumber, fennel, and zucchini on the mandoline and toss with the dressing.

2. Shred the kale into thin strips with a knife and toss with the other veggies. Let marinate at least 30 minutes and up to 1 hour before serving.

3. Break up the lettuce by hand into bite-sized pieces and place in a large salad bowl.

4. Toss in the marinated shredded vegetables and top with the sweet peas and the sunflower sprouts.

Basic Chopped Salad

Growing up in Beachwood, Ohio, my grandparents would often take me to lunch at their country club. I loved to go there with them as it was always a grand experience and the waiters knew just what we wanted without our even ordering. The chopped salad was my favorite and it was served with a sweet poppy seed dressing. I think I really loved the salad because I could eat it with a spoon and this was fun for me. The chopped salad is a familiar feature on most menus now, and they always make me feel nostalgic for my grandparents, Beechmont Country Club, and the bright yellow poppy seed dressing.

Chopping a salad only requires an oversized cutting board, a big knife or two (as many Japanese chefs do), OR a $1/2$ round knife. There is no rule as to what vegetables you have to use, so a chopped salad is a great way to use up extra vegetables and even leftovers. Personally, I try to vary the crunch factor (the crunchier the better) and many veggies scream to be chopped.

Some examples of these are:

- Celery root
- Beet
- Carrots
- Romaine lettuce
- Cauliflower
- Parsnips
- Cabbage
- Green beans

For other toppings to add or chop:

- Avocado
- Seaweed
- Black olives
- Raisins or sultanas
- Almonds or nut of choice

Great additions for carnivores:

- Cheese
- Eggs
- Chicken
- Tuna
- Or any protein of choice

I would give possible salad combinations here, but I like to force people to be creative and try unusual combinations of ingredients. Chopped salads are incredibly user-friendly and very difficult to mess up.

- Cucumbers chop best when de-seeded. Cut the cucumber in half length-wise and scrape the seeds out with a spoon.

- Peppers, carrots, celery, onions, and most firm veggies chop best when already roughly sliced or roughly chopped.

- Make sure that olives are pitted before chopping.

- Tomatoes are a difficult addition, as they can get mushy and wet down the whole salad.

- Try to mix two types of lettuce, one crispy (romaine or iceberg) and one softer (butter or mache). This gives the salad good texture and base for the salad to sit on.

- Sticking with a maximum of 4 or 5 additions is a good amount. Too many ingredients can overwhelm the salad with too many confusing flavors.

The Swirly Salad

The Swirly Salad name is mine; the concept unreservedly from Asian cooking. There is a kitchen tool called the spiralizer that helps create noodles out of practically anything. The Asians have been swirling for decades and most people look at the swirls of daikon and carrot served alongside sushi as garnish. Spiralizing is an entertaining way to incorporate veggies. Kids love the noodle-like veg because it's like playing with your food. It's the kids who have it right and the grownups who kid themselves into being serious about it. You can also take your swirly vegetable noodles, toss some pasta sauce on top, and *voila*—raw pasta! Spiralizers cost around thirty dollars. I personally have a Benriner, but most of the Asian brands are very good.

The most successful vegetable swirls are made with a firm root vegetable like daikon, squash, zucchini, beet, or carrot. Some other good vegetables to swirl are sweet potato, cucumber, celery root, jicama, and yam.

Swirly salads are easy to put together and to mix and match, depending on what is in season and what is available.

INGREDIENTS

1 daikon, swirled

1 sweet potato, swirled

1. Lightly cut the swirls so the strands are not too long.

2. Toss with dressing of choice or one from Chapter Two. If swirling vegetable pasta—try pesto or tomato cashew. If tossing over green leaves—marinate the veggie noodles in dressing for at least 30 minutes before tossing into leaves.

A CARNIVORE'S CHOICE

* Excellent with tuna plus pesto
* Raw sushi salmon
* Hard boiled egg

Salad 101

Salad bars are popping up all over the world. Creating your own *fridge* salad bar is just as easy. The inspiration for this came from a stylist client who wanted to make her own salads but didn't want to chop or clean, and she ate when I wasn't around to do these things for her. Because she was a stylist, it had to be pleasing to the eye. I bought her a dozen short and wide Le Parfait jars to keep in the fridge, and I pre-chopped each ingredient so she could have variety and choice to build her salad from a green leafy base.

THINGS TO ADD IN AND ON A "GREEN SALAD"

Julienne Beet	Sweet Pea Shoots	Red Bell Pepper
Carrot	Tomato	Radicchio
Cucumber	Dulse Sheets	Endive
Daikon	Sweet Peas	Black or Green Olives
Jicama	Wakame	Sliced Fennel
Scallions	Avocado	Chopped Garlic
Red Onion	Hemp Seeds	Sliced Zucchini
Asparagus	Chopped Kale	Nori Sheets

CHAPTER SIX

Roasted, Baked, and Sautéed Small Plates

The concept and inspiration behind small dishes comes from two main sources. The first is the Mediterranean tradition of "Meze," which consists of eating several small dishes to comprise a larger meal. Similarly, in Italy the tradition called Aperativo has become widely popular. The bars serve many plates to nibble on while having drinks before dinner. The bars often serve such an immense array of scrumptious treats that one can easily make this a substitute for dinner. My friends and I would spend hours nursing a single glass of Prosecco wine and picking on a mammoth pile of roasted fennel, farro salads, bruschetta, and loads of other delectable treats. The question of dinner never seemed to come up.

Small plates are pieces to the larger puzzle of putting together a complete meal or a vegetarian feast. They are also an exemplary accompaniment for any carnivorous dish and are perfect platforms for most of the dressings, dips, and sauces that have made up the bulk of the prior recipes. This is where creative juices can *flow* and my suggestions are most certainly only a guideline.

Roasting or steaming are my methods of choice for cooking veggies. The flavors intensify, the veggies get sweeter, and the nutritional value remains constant. The Baseball Technique (outlined in this chapter) makes roasting practically foolproof with its ease of preparation.

Just about any vegetable can be roasted and turned into a refrigerator staple to be kept on hand to enhance other dishes. Roasted garlic or peppers are a good example of this. You can keep roasted garlic in the fridge for up to a week to add into other dishes. Chopped up roasted vegetables are beautiful additions to a raw salad or as a topping for any protein.

When roasting or sautéing, the oil or fat in which you choose to cook your veggies will alter the taste. In addition, certain oils have higher burning points, so a saturated fat like coconut oil, cacao butter, or organic butter are the ones I mainly use.

As I have mentioned before, different oils serve different needs. I have found that cooking the veggies in a small amount of coconut oil deepens the flavor of the veggie without adding too much coconut flavor. Olive oil can be added later to get the full flavor and nutritional value of the oil. I picked up that piece of information in Spain while watching the cooks at the market sauté calamari. Raw oil tastes cleaner and purer and is better for digestion. Organic butter is also a superb choice for roasting or sautéing.

Recipes Included in This Chapter

Sformato di Spinach

Edamame Succotash

Sandhya's Chili-Seared Green Beans

Roasted Root Fries

Cauliflower Steak with Harissa Sauce

Ratatouille

Zucchini Carpaccio

Crudité

Millet Tabbouleh

Grilled Baby Romaine and Radicchio Salad

Corn Fritters with Shredded Veggies

Baseball Method of Roasting Veggies

Coconut-Roasted Vegetables

Coconut-Roasted Cauliflower

Coconut-Roasted Broccoli

Vatican Greens

Stuffed Egg Crepes

Sformato di Spinach

Shopping one day in Napoli I found a tiny, very chic shop on the edge of the Spanish district. I noticed it because of the oversized Buddha in the window. The clothes were fantastic, but what really caught my eye was the yoga schedule on the wall next to David Woolf's famous raw-foods book, *Conscious Eating*. In my best Italian, I asked the shopkeeper if she was a vegetarian. She was so excited that I knew about David Woolf's book, and we chatted for nearly an hour about vegetables, nutrition, juicing, and eating in Italy. She suggested a place for lunch where she ate often that made outstanding vegetables. The tiny trattoria had a huge array of vegetables of all sorts: roasted onions, steamed broccoli raab, grilled eggplant—I could go on and on. One item on the buffet confused me. I wasn't sure if it was an omelet or a frittata. The restaurant owner corrected me and introduced me to the sformato (or "form"), which is an omelet-type/soufflé-type of egg and vegetable dish that can be made with any puréed or chopped vegetable. This recipe calls for spinach, but after you make it once, you will see that you can replace the spinach with anything you have on hand.

I use Pecorino Toscana (an Italian goat cheese from Tuscany). I like the salty taste and find it complements the neutral spinach.

INGREDIENTS

3 pounds spinach, rinsed well

Pinch of cinnamon

Salt and pepper

2 Tbsp. salt
(for water to boil spinach)

1 Tbsp. organic butter,
plus more for greasing casserole
(or coconut oil)

3 beaten eggs

$^1/_2$ cup freshly grated Pecorino Toscana

1. Preheat the oven to 375 degrees F.

2. Bring 6 quarts of water to a boil and add 2 tablespoons salt. Add the spinach and cook for 30 seconds, until just limp. Drain, squeeze out the excess moisture, and chop finely.

3. Place the spinach in the bowl of a blender or food processor and purée with the cinnamon, salt, and pepper. Turn the purée out into a bowl, add the butter, eggs, and cheese and stir well.

4. Turn the mixture into a well-buttered casserole and cook in the oven for 15 to 20 minutes, until the eggs are set and the top is golden brown.

5. Cut into wedges and serve hot.

VARIATIONS AND TIPS

- It's important to get the texture right or the custard will have a very odd consistency.
- A blender works best for this recipe.
- This is excellent topped with the harissa sauce or the red pepper sauce.
- Almost any vegetable can be used in this recipe!

A CARNIVORE'S CHOICE

- Bresaola or tuna can be added to the top of the sformato.

Edamame Succotash

Serve alone, over fish, or on top of a big green salad.

INGREDIENTS

1 zucchini, diced

1 yellow squash, diced

1 small sweet potato, diced

1 small ear of organic corn,
cut off the cob and blanched

$^3/_4$ cup edamame, blanched

Salt and pepper to taste

Crushed red pepper to taste

1. Preheat the oven to 350 and line a baking sheet with parchment paper.

2. Toss the zucchini, yellow squash, and sweet potato in salt, pepper, and a small amount of melted butter.

3. Roast for 30 minutes or until soft and a bit brown.

4. In the meantime, blanch the corn and the edamame in salted boiling water and drain.

5. Toss together and season with salt, pepper, and crushed red pepper.

VARIATIONS

- Almost any vegetable will work in a succotash.
- The only constant is the edamame and the corn so this is a perfect recipe to use lone vegetables that are leftover in the veggie drawer.
- Please experiment!

Sandhya's Chili-Seared Green Beans

There is an elegant lady in Mysore, India, named Sandhya who runs an in-home restaurant and rents rooms to yoga students. I was fortunate to be one of those students. The rooms were modest, and we had to climb down a ladder to get to the loo and the showers, but I loved it. This was my first stay in Southern India, and I didn't need much more. Sandhya's House was filled every day with hungry yoga practitioners waiting for her food. Reservations were always necessary—even for me, and I lived there. She served some of the most delicious vegetarian food I have ever tasted, even to this day. The food went fast at her table. Sandhya's mastery of vegetables is enviable, and I feel so grateful that she let me observe her cooking and shop the markets with her. While Sandhya is a woman of few words, her facial expressions said it all. If something was not turning out to her liking she made one expression; if the chai was not boiling properly, she made another—she had a penchant for subtleness. This is an adaptation of one of her recipes.

INGREDIENTS

1 pound green beans or haricot vert
(elongated, French green beans), ends trimmed

$1/2$ Tbsp. organic butter or coconut oil

Crushed red pepper flakes to taste

Salt and pepper to taste

1. Cook the trimmed beans in a large pot of boiling, very salted water.

2. Cook until bright green or about 4 minutes and drain.

3. Plunge the beans into ice water to stop the cooking.

4. Heat a large cast iron skillet (or any large skillet) and add $1/2$ Tbsp. of organic butter or coconut oil. (Note: I don't use any oil on the beans at all when I am using a cast iron skillet as I find that they get a better sear.)

5. Sear the beans, sprinkling generously with the red pepper.

6. Adding olive oil at the finish is optional.

VARIATIONS

- Try substituting asparagus, sweet peas, or broccoli raab.
- You can use green beans instead of haricot vert.

Roasted Root Fries

My friend Michelle and I declared French-fries a gift from heaven when we were traveling in Greece several years back. We simply couldn't eat enough of them, as they tasted so light, fresh, and much better than any French-fries either of us had ever tasted before. We were stuck on a random little island due to weather conditions. I asked the cook at our favorite beachside tavern how they were prepared. She sort of laughed at me almost as if to say "How else?" and pointed to a bottle of olive oil. Michelle and I pretty much made lunch or dinner out of a green salad and Greek fries and were in heaven. Back home I tried to replicate them, with little success. I realized that in addition to the olive oil, the way they spiced the potatoes set them apart. Often tossing them in oregano or fresh lime, the potatoes were extra crispy and often fried or baked along with the herbs to make them crunchy. I extended the recipe to include some of my favorite roots, along with the herbs—all cooked Greek style.

INGREDIENTS

2 large beets cut into wedges

2 Tbsp. olive oil

$1/2$ Tbsp. coconut oil for greasing pan

1. Oil a cookie sheet with the coconut oil and toss the beet wedges in one Tbsp. of the olive oil. Sprinkle with sea salt.

2. Bake at 375 for around 45 minutes, tossing midway through. The roots are done when they are crisp but not burned.

INGREDIENTS FOR SPICE MIXTURE

1 Tbsp. lime zest

1Tbsp. crushed red chili flakes

2 Tbsp. sea salt

1. Put the zest, chili flakes, and sea salt in a coffee grinder and buzz for about 30 seconds, or until blended. A mortar and pestle works just as well. Sprinkle over the hot fries and toss well.

VARIATIONS

- These fries pair deliciously with the horseradish dip.
- You can speed the cooking process by pre-boiling the beets for 5–10 minutes.
- Alternate fries: Sweet potato, white potato, purple potato, carrot, parsnip.

Cauliflower Steak with Harissa Sauce

I once saw cauliflower steak on a menu in Miami, and it excited me immensely—mainly because I couldn't imagine what it could be. I had high hopes but was sorely disappointed when my large slice of cauliflower was served piled high with three different sauces and a few varieties of nuts. I scraped until I could taste the perfectly grilled veggie. The spicy harissa sauce is my preference, but any of the dressings or dips will go well with this.

INGREDIENTS

1 large cauliflower

Chopped parsley for topping

Paprika (optional)

Harissa sauce:

1 medium red bell pepper, whole

$1/4$ teaspoon cumin (I like more)

$1/4$ teaspoon coriander

$1/4$ teaspoon caraway

1 Tbsp. olive oil

1 small red onion, roughly chopped

1 jalapeno chili, diced

1 serrano pepper, diced (I like the sauce hotter, so I use 2)

2 large cloves garlic, smashed

2 Tbsp. tomato paste

$1/2$ lemon, juiced

1 Tbsp. nama shoyu or soy sauce (or tamari for gluten-free)

1 tsp. sea salt (or salt to taste)

1. Cut the bottom off the cauliflower, trying to keep the entire flower and core intact.

2. Stand it on end and slice it in $1/4$ to $1/2$-inch-thick slices.

3. Salt and pepper well and sprinkle with paprika (optional).

Three methods of cooking the cauliflower:

1. **In a pan on the stove:** Heat the pan on medium high and add a small amount of organic butter or coconut oil and a tiny amount of olive oil until hot. Sear the steaks on each side until well—colored. This takes about 3 minutes per side.

2. **On a grill:** In this method, you will want to rub the sliced cauliflower with a small amount of olive oil.

3. **Broil in the oven:** Heat the oven to 400 degrees and place the sliced cauliflower on a lined cookie sheet and broil for about 7 minutes per side.

To make the harissa:

1. If you have a gas stove, skewer the bell pepper and roast it directly on the gas flame, turning it every minute or two until the entire surface is blackened. If you do not have a gas stove, put the pepper under a broiler to brown.

2. When black, set aside until cool and then run under water to peel the blackened skin off.

3. Toast all the spices in a pan over medium high heat until fragrant (about a minute).

4. Add the tablespoon of olive oil to a skillet with the red onion, chilies, and garlic; stir until translucent and browned, about 7–8 minutes. Set aside to cool.

5. Core, remove seeds, and dice red pepper.

6. In a food processor or blender, combine the red bell pepper, ground spices, onion, garlic, and chili with the remaining harissa ingredients and process until smooth. Set aside until needed.

7. Top the cooked cauliflower with lots of harissa, chopped parsley, and sea salt.

Ratatouille

About an hour or so north of Aix en Provence in the south of France is a tiny town called Lacoste. There is a small oak grove where Van Gogh used to do ink drawings, and a castle in ruins overlooking the village where the Marquis de Sade used to live. There is also a petit, yet well-respected art school I attended for two months the summer before I went to university. I spoke no French, had never been to France before, and given it was the late 80s, I was still wearing blue mascara, bearing a striking resemblance to Madonna. Everyone at the school was an established art student and already in university. I befriended a local Parisian girl named Sophie, who was not enrolled in the program; her family had a house in the little town. Sophie was quintessentially Parisian and in my Midwestern eyes, couldn't be more glamorous or cool. She wore no makeup except for lipstick, she had real lingerie, and she smoked and drank espresso. During my early "French education process," she also took me to the only two restaurants in the village. Having never eaten in a traditional French restaurant before, I had no idea what I was in for or actually how good the food was. The chef and owner of the restaurant with seating for ten made one meal a night with one choice of wine. That night the first course was ratatouille with a big basket of crunchy, fresh baguette. Sophie rolled her eyes. "Peasant food," she said. But I was in heaven.

INGREDIENTS

1 large onion, diced

2 cloves garlic, smashed

1 or 2 eggplants, cubed (depending on how much you like eggplant)

2 zucchini, diced

1 red pepper, diced

1 yellow pepper, diced

8–10 cherry tomatoes

2 Tbsp. fresh parsley leaves, chopped

2 Tbsp. fresh rosemary, chopped

2 Tbsp. fresh thyme, chopped

2 Tbsp. fresh basil, chopped

Salt and pepper to taste

About $1/4$ cup olive oil plus 2 Tbsp. organic butter (or coconut oil for vegan option)

1. Put the eggplant in a colander and salt well. Toss and let sit to drain. (See Fascinating Tip about aubergine.)

2. Press the water out after about an hour. Rinse with water and press again with paper towels; make sure to dry well. The eggplant will discolor and mush. This is okay.

3. Preheat the oven to 475 degrees.

4. Oil a cookie sheet with a bit of the organic butter or coconut oil. Toss the eggplant, peppers, and zucchini in some of the olive oil. Season with salt and pepper. Roast for about 30 minutes, stirring halfway through.

5. In a large heavy-bottomed pot, heat about 3 Tbsp. of oil and 1 Tbsp. of butter and sauté the onions until clear. Add the garlic for about 20 seconds and then the tomatoes. Cook for about 5–7 minutes.

6. Add the vegetables from the oven and combine well.

7. Add the herbs and let all of the flavors combine. Adjust with salt and pepper.

8. This is much better the next day. Reheat on the stove.

FASCINATING FACTS/TIPS

- Aubergine (eggplant) is a very watery veggie and needs to be dried before roasting.

- To salt and get the excess water out of the eggplant, put the cubed vegetable in a colander and place over a bowl. Sprinkle with salt and toss well. Let it sit and absorb the salt.

- Press the eggplant with paper towels or a clean towel to remove the water.

- The eggplant will shrink.

Zucchini Carpaccio

The Red Cat in New York is one of my favorite restaurants. Jimmy Bradley, the owner and brilliant chef, has a dish on his menu called "Quick Sear of Zucchini with Pecorino" that has always been one of my favorites. It has been on the menu for over 13 years, and it still tastes just as fresh as it did the first time I had it. I once asked Jimmy how he made it, and he looked at me like I was crazy (or dumb). His reply was, "It's a quick sear of zucchini with pecorino, salt, and pepper." These are almost the same ingredients, but with my raw twist on his classic.

INGREDIENTS

2 small green zucchinis, sliced thin

2 small yellow squash, sliced thin

$1/2$ cup basil leaves

2 Tbsp. olive oil (plus a splash more to drizzle on top)

2 Tbsp. lemon juice (lime is also delicious on this)

Sea salt and pepper to taste

Large handful (about 1cup) of arugula

5 ounces Pecorino Romano
(or parmigan/parmesan if that is your preference)

1. Slice zucchini diagonally into thin slices with mandoline.

2. Arrange them on the plate so they overlap.

3. Sprinkle the basil leaves over the veggies.

4. Top with combined olive oil and lemon juice; sprinkle generously with sea salt and black pepper.

5. Allow the flavors to marinate and soften for at least 20 minutes.

6. Toss the arugula leaves with the remainder of the olive oil and lemon juice and place on top of the zucchini to serve.

7. Delicious served with shaved Pecorino Romano.

- Substitute with mushroom, carrot, radish, beet.
- Any firm vegetable that can be sliced with the mandoline.
- Shave any cheese or vegan cheese on top.

Crudité

There is an art to a good crudité platter. As I quickly discovered in France, "Salad Crudité" is an assortment of raw veggies and most often will consist of very few leaves. Normally, endive is on the plate. France is where I discovered endive as a dipper, and it is the perfect dipper as it is already scoop-shaped.

CRUDITÉ 101

VEGGIES TO PUT IN A CRUDITÉ ASSORTMENT

Bell Peppers	Cucumber	Radicchio Wedge
Cabbage Wedge	Endive	Radish
Carrots	Fennel	Scallions
Cauliflower	Gem Lettuce Wedge	Snow Peas
Celery	Haricot Vert or Green Beans	Yellow Squash
Celery Root	Jicama	Zucchini Spears

Arrange the veggies on a platter OR I like to put them in little individual cups. The vegetable that will stand up (celery, zucchini, carrot sticks, etc.) will look pretty with the other vegetables placed around it.

Millet Tabbouleh

INGREDIENTS

3/4 cup millet

One vegetable bouillon cube

2 cups fresh, flat leaf parsley, chopped

3 scallions, sliced

1 sweet red bell pepper, diced

1 English cucumber, diced (remove the seeds first—
see Fascinating Fact about cucumbers)

Juice of one lemon

1/3 cup olive oil

Pinch of cinnamon

1 tsp. crushed red pepper flakes
(or more if you like it spicy)

1 tsp. sumac (if you don't have sumac,
use one Tbsp. of lemon zest)

Salt and pepper to taste

Handful (about 8) grape tomatoes, sliced in quarters

1. Add the millet to 2 cups boiling water and 1 vegetable bouillon cube.

2. Cover, reduce the heat, and let simmer for about 20 minutes. Remove the cover, fluff, and let cool. The millet should be on the firm side, not mushy.

3. For the dressing, mix the olive oil, lemon, spices, and salt and allow the flavors to blend.

4. When the millet is cool, add half the dressing and toss. Be sure to add the dressing slowly, making sure not to soak the grains.

5. Add the parsley, onion, bell pepper, and cucumber and toss lightly.

6. Check for taste to adjust seasonings and the amount of dressing. You may have to adjust the seasoning depending on how spicy you like it. I like my tabbouleh fairly light.

7. Add the tomatoes last, as they get mushy. I like to serve them on top, but some like them tossed in.

8. This recipe is even better the next day.

FASCINATING FACT/TIP

To remove the seeds from the cucumber, slice the cucumber in half lengthwise and run a spoon along the middle to scoop the seeds out. This prevents the salad from getting mushy.

Grilled Baby Romaine and Radicchio Salad

Sometimes the worst experiences prove to have the sweetest outcomes. A friend from Paris invited me to go on holiday with his group of friends who grew up together in Marseilles. We rented a big house in a very small town in Northern Italy. I speak passable Parisian French, but this group was composed of Southern French speakers. Their accents were vastly different from anything I could understand. Frustrated with being unable to communicate with the group, I wandered off into the little town and sat at a small outdoor café. I must have been sitting for hours and drank several pots of tea before ordering anything to eat. I watched almost every dish on the menu as it was brought out, so by the time I decided to order I knew exactly what I wanted to try.

INGREDIENTS

1 head romaine lettuce, split in quarters

2 heads radicchio split lengthwise, keeping root intact

Olive oil

Crushed red pepper to taste (Paprika is also delicious.)

Salt and pepper to taste

1. Brush the lettuce with olive oil and sprinkle with salt and pepper.

2. Broil on high for about 5 minutes, turning as it browns.

3. Top with more salt and pepper, olive oil, and crushed red pepper.

VARIATIONS

- Endive or any other firm lettuce with a thick root can be substituted.

- For carnivores, top with Italian tuna, boiled egg, or anchovies.

Corn Fritters
with Shredded Veggies

Take a woman from the Deep South and have her cook for a Kosher Jewish family in Cleveland, Ohio, and she is bound to come up with some creative dishes. Doris, my grandmother's cleaning woman, cook, and mostly companion, was the chef of the house and I loved her food. We had dinner at my grandmother's house every Friday, and I couldn't wait for Fridays. One of our favorites was her corn fritters served with maple syrup. They were hot, fluffy pillows that crunched on the outside and we ate them with our fingers.

INGREDIENTS

1 beet, shredded

2 carrots, shredded

1 or 2 zucchini, shredded

2 ears fresh corn, kernels cut off cob and blended or mashed well

2 eggs, whipped

2 Tbsp. (or more) coconut oil or butter

Salt and pepper to taste

1. Blend the corn with the egg in a blender and toss all of the vegetables in the batter.

2. Heat a skillet on medium high and add coconut oil or butter.

3. Spoon about 2 Tbsp. of the batter onto the hot skillet (pancake size) and fry the fritters until brown.

4. Flip over and cook on the other side.

5. Top with yogurt/tzatziki sauce, maple syrup, or is also excellent with the horseradish sauce.

VARIATION

- This is also delicious spiced with curry powder or garam masala.

Baseball Method of Roasting Veggies

This must be the easiest and most nutritious way to roast veggies. The veggies are wrapped like baseballs and tossed in the oven. Cooking time will vary a bit depending on what is being roasted.

1. Wrap the veggie in foil or parchment (or place in a tightly sealed baking dish or clay pot).

2. Roast at 375 for around 40 (plus or minus) minutes. Lightly squeeze the veggie to see if it is soft. It's best not to let them get too mushy or they are hard to work with and are over-cooked. If you roast them whole, you can slice them as you prefer after they are cooked.

FASCINATING FACTS

- **Roasting asparagus, carrot, parsnip, etc. will require less roasting time than a potato or beet.**

- **When roasting in foil, you really do not need any fat at all. However, if you rub a bit of coconut oil or butter on the vegetable it will, of course, taste exceptional.**

ROASTING VEGETABLES

Vegetable	Preparation	Cooking Time
Asparagus	trim, snap bottom off	30 min
Artichoke	slice in quarters	40 min
Beet	whole or half	40 min +
Brussels sprouts	halved	25 min
Carrot	whole or sliced	30 min
Cauliflower	trim	30 min
Fennel	trim, whole	30 min
Jerusalem artichoke	clean, whole	30 min
Onions	trim, half or quarter	30–40 min
Potatoes	whole	40 min +
Parsnip	trim, whole or slice	30 min
Pumpkin	slice	30 min

Cococnut-Roasted Vegetables

Coconut-roasting is a simple technique with exceptional results. The veggies always end up flavorful and impressive. Any vegetable can be cooked this way, either on a cookie sheet or in a baking dish. The cookie sheet gives the veggie room to crisp, whereas the baking dish may cause steaming due to crowding. It is just a different result.

1. Line 1 or 2 large cookie sheets with parchment paper.

2. Oil the parchment with coconut oil or organic butter.

3. Arrange the veggies on the cookie sheet and sprinkle with a small amount salt and olive oil.

Coconut-Roasted Cauliflower

INGREDIENTS

1 head cauliflower, broken up into florets

1 Tbsp. coconut oil

1Tbsp. olive oil plus a small amount for the finish

Salt and pepper to taste

1. Preheat the oven to 375 degrees. Line a cookie sheet with parchment paper and oil with coconut oil.

2. Lay the cauliflower out on the cookie sheet and toss in olive oil, making sure the cauliflower gets some of the coconut oil on it.

3. Sprinkle with the salt and pepper and small amount of olive oil.

4. Roast for about 35–40 minutes, tossing occasionally to be sure not to burn the florets.

Coconut-Roasted Broccoli

INGREDIENTS

1 head broccoli, broken up into florets

1 Tbsp. coconut oil

1Tbsp. olive oil

1 lime, zested

Salt and pepper to taste

1. Preheat the oven to 375 degrees. Line a cookie sheet parchment paper and oil with coconut oil.

2. Lay the broccoli out on the cookie sheet and toss in olive oil, making sure the broccoli gets some of the coconut oil on it.

3. Sprinkle with salt, pepper, and lime zest.

4. Roast for about 35–40 minutes, occasionally tossing the florets.

VARIATIONS

- Use Moroccan spices on the broccoli.

- Try roasting carrot batons and season with cumin.

- Try roasting Brussels sprouts and sprinkle with nama shoyu.

- Roast asparagus and toss in lime zest.

Vatican Greens

My friend in Rome had a lovely girlfriend named Federica whose hobby was being a tour guide. She spoke six languages and was a history major in university, so this seemed the perfect job for her. One weekend when a friend from New York was visiting, she offered to give us a tour of the Vatican. We jumped at the opportunity to be shown the Vatican by a pro. Federica led us to the front of the line, zipping past several thousand patient tourists. We spent hours inside the grand museum. It was surreal. I had been there once before when I was fifteen, but only remembered the tombs of the past Popes. I hadn't remembered the halls of artwork and intricate details on the walls. Had we not been with Federica, we would not have spent the time exploring the Colonnades or even known that Bernini designed both the courtyard and the figures that lined the corridors—162 of them, according to Federica and the book she gave us. After our extensive tour, we walked back through Vatican City and down the tiny streets of Rome. We ended up in a charming little restaurant that she said was one of her favorites. Federica was a friend of the owner, who wanted to make us a special lunch—pasta, of course. She explained to him that I didn't eat pasta, but would like to have a plate of greens. He looked at me oddly, but was happy to accommodate. His greens were outrageous. So much so that I thought he made them with some type of lard or bacon, but he said no. He took me into the kitchen and showed me how he made them.

INGREDIENTS

1½–2 pounds broccoli raab

2 cloves garlic
(chopped or shredded on a microplane)

1 lemon, zested

1 teaspoon crushed red pepper
(or pepperoncino)

1. Fill a medium pot with water and salt and bring to a boil. Add the broccoli raab and boil for about 2 minutes until it turns bright green. Do not overcook. Drain well and run under cold water or plunge in an ice bath.

2. Preheat a sauté pan and add a small amount of butter or coconut oil. Add the garlic and sauté for about 20–30 seconds. Add the broccoli raab and heat through. Top with olive oil, red pepper flakes, and lemon zest. Toss well.

VARIATIONS

- This recipe can be made with any other greens: collards, escarole, kale, etc.

SAUTÉED SPINACH

I never use oil to heat spinach. I only heat the pan, wilt the spinach, then add the oil and zest after. Spinach is very tricky and will shrink quickly due to its high water content.

Stuffed Egg Crepes

There are very few foods in France that are appropriate *standing* or *walking* foods—crepes and ice cream are two of them. This is one of the many things I love about France: food and meals are a ritual, and even when it comes to taking a coffee, one sits and takes the time to enjoy it. Although I didn't eat all that many crepes, as they are made with white flour, I did embrace the savory crepe, or galette. Made with buckwheat, it is gluten-free. My favorite place in Paris to have galette was a crepe stand near the Odéon Metro. They make almost any combination you can think of. My preference was one stuffed with arugula, goat cheese, and artichoke, with lots of hot red pepper.

INGREDIENTS

3 organic eggs

Splash of water

Salt and pepper to taste

1. Whisk the eggs together well with the water and season.

2. Heat a sauté pan on medium high and add a small amount of organic butter. Be sure to cover the entire pan. This works best with a non-stick pan or crepe pan, but any sauté pan will do.

3. Ladle just enough of the egg mixture to coat the bottom of the sauté pan. It should be thin, but not too thin.

4. After about a minute, use a rubber spatula to loosen the sides and flip over.

5. Cook through and put the crepe on a plate. Fill with whatever filling you have chosen or with just with a little maple syrup and salt.

VARIATIONS

Here are some possible fillings for crepes. Top with any of the dressings.

- Sautéed greens
- Chopped salad
- Shredded salad

- Edamame Succotash
- Ratatouille

CHAPTER SEVEN

Smoothies, Tonics, and Potions

A mericans love drinks. We walk around with bottles, take-out cups, and plastic drink holders as though it's our right. The interesting part about this is that most Americans are dehydrated. Oddly enough, the rest of the world embraces water, doesn't walk around with take-out cups and bottles, and does not have as much of a dehydration issue. For me to get my American clients and friends to drink pure water is quite a task. However, I have found ways around this and many of them are quite tasty.

Smoothies, Tonics, and Potions are mostly concoctions I have made for clients and friends in order to satisfy their sweet tooth and make sure they stay hydrated. Many can be used as a snack, breakfast, or even as a light meal. The main ingredients are coconut water (preferably fresh, but see source list) nut milk, greens, nuts, fruit, and fruit juices. The primary sweeteners are honey, coconut sugar (also called palm sugar), date water, and maple syrup. I encourage you to play around with these. Most of the tonics are complemented by a shot of tequila, rum, or even vodka.

FASCINATING FACT

Glycemic Index of Unrefined Sugars:

A glycemic index (GI) gives the carbohydrate content of foods and was essentially developed for diabetics to help keep their insulin regulated. It is quite useful. The less you "spike" your blood sugar with high GI, refined foods such as white processed sugar, bread, and pastas, the more consistent your appetite and energy levels will be.

Recipes Included in This Chapter

Ginger Lime Tonic

Mojito Tonic

Frozen Mojito Pops

English Breakfast Iced Tea
with Sage Ice Cubes

Cold Filtered Coffee with Coffee Ice Cubes
(Deli Guy's Cold Brew Coffee)

Lazy Days Nut Milk

Chocolate-Peanut Butter Milk

The Basic Nut Milk Recipe

Thick Coconut Milkshake
with Vanilla Bean

Vegetable Juice

Salad Juice

Winter Tan Juice

Indian Masala Chai

Chai Spiced Smoothie

Ginger Lime Tonic

Known in Hindi as Nimbu Pani, this lime-water quickly became my drink of choice in India. On my first visit, I was up north and our host ordered me one from the Nimbu Pani Wala (lime water guy) who asked if I wanted it salty or sweet. I chose a sweet one and in classic Indian style, it was extremely sweet. However, I was hooked. I befriended the Nimbu Pani Wala near my apartment in Delhi who showed me how to combine the salt and the sweet to create a balanced and truly hydrating drink. I began bringing him different forms of sugar to try, which he found odd, but he humored me and we finally found a brew that I loved. It was made with jaggery, which is similar to the taste of molasses. He made the refreshing drink my way every morning.

INGREDIENTS

2 limes, juiced

1 lemon, juiced

1–2 Tbsp. maple syrup
or coconut sugar

1" piece of fresh ginger, juiced or grated
(or $1/2$ Tbsp. ginger powder)

Pinch of salt

Handful of ice

1.5 liters of water

1. Place all the ingredients in a blender, including the ice.

2. Whip until the ice is crushed and sweetener is incorporated. (You can add more sweetener if you desire, or more water. This is a very basic recipe that is meant to be customized according to the sweetener of your choice.)

"JUICING" GINGER

One way to get the juice out of ginger is to "grate" the root on a microplane or porcelain ginger grater. The root needs to be gently peeled first. After grating, you can put the ginger gratings in a piece of cheesecloth and squeeze the juice out. Alternatively, you can use the grating as is for a stronger flavor.

Mojito Tonic

This hydrating and refreshing tonic was inspired by a client who did not like to drink water. It can be difficult to force anyone to drink or eat anything, but I have learned over the years that certain flavors will spark certain responses in particular palates. This was a man who loved the beach and loved a good strong Mojito. Since rum was not part of his cleanse, we came up with a compromise fresh from his garden. Citrus is consistently refreshing and mint is a natural aid for digestion. The longer the tonic sits, the stronger it gets. It can be made without a juicer, but always in a blender.

INGREDIENTS

2–3 liters of water

3 cups ice cubes

Juice of 2 lemons

Juice of 2 limes

Small bunch of mint

1 Tbsp. maple or honey (optional, adjust sweetener to your taste)

1. Put in a blender and blend like crazy. Should be slushy.

FROZEN MOJITO POPS

Freeze the Mojito Tonic in ice cube trays or little Dixie cups with Popsicle sticks for frozen treats. You may want to add extra sweetener—when anything is frozen, it tends to lose its sweetness.

English Breakfast Iced Tea with Sage Ice Cubes

Tea and coffee are easy ways to engage and embrace a foreign culture. I've always found that when invited for one or the other, I'm able to snatch a vivid glimpse into what's more than just a caffeine fix. For example, in India when I was offered a short cup of sweet-spicy-milky tea in the late afternoon with the sun beating down and the temperature well over 90, I began to understand how, instead of causing one to feel even hotter, spices and hot drinks can be medicinal and cooling in the heat.

A few summers ago I was scuba diving in the Sinai Peninsula; it was hot, windy, and next to impossible to cool down except when we were in the water. Not only did I not want to eat, but I found that the only thing I really wanted to drink was the sage tea that the local beach restaurants offered. In the Middle East, hot tea is made from black tea and dried sage leaves. Sage is a natural coolant and has been used for centuries to help regulate body temperature as well as aid hydration and digestion.

Because sage is also known to ward off evil spirits, plus negative and stale energy, I just assumed that drinking it or burning it would have similar effects. So I asked. It seems that the gentlemen traveling the desert *did* actually use the sage tea as a protective shield of sorts against the evil spirits there.

The healing properties of this leaf run deep. Not only can gargling with a sage infusion help with a sore throat, mouth ulcers, and halitosis, but drinking a strong infusion on a regular basis can actually help to alleviate anxiety and depression, as well as sharpen memory. I would suggest that you pot a plant of it immediately and start reaping the benefits.

INGREDIENTS

3 bags of English Breakfast Tea (or any black tea)

2 oz. dried sage leaves (I like to put them in tea bags)

2 quarts water (or more, depending on
how much tea and how big your pitchers are)

1. Place tea bags in one pot or jar, and sage leaves in another. (I like to use large Mason jars.)

2. Boil the water.

3. Pour the water over the bags in each jar and let steep for at least an hour. (I like a very strong brew for iced tea and especially for iced tea cubes.)

4. The sage can brew for up to 3 hours without getting bitter.

5. Remove the bags and let cool.

6. When the tea has cooled, fill ice cube trays with the sage brew and freeze.

7. Serve the black tea with a large handful of sage ice cubes.

Cold Filtered Coffee
with Coffee Ice Cubes
(Deli Guy's Cold Brew Coffee)

When the weather turns hot in Manhattan, it turns fast. One of my favorite treats when I was in school at Parsons School of Design in New York was deli iced coffee. For some reason, it just tasted better there. With a little investigation, I found out why: the owner of the deli made his coffee with a cold brew. The difference between a cold brew and coffee that is brewed and put over ice is night and day. A true cold brew is full of flavor and on the sweeter side with absolutely no bitterness and never tastes watered down. The interesting thing about a cold brew is that it contains less caffeine and less acid than a hot brew. The result is generally much smoother and sweeter tasting. The deli guy explained to me that it needs to be steeped like a tea overnight to make a coffee concentrate. To serve, hot or cool water is added to it. He brewed all of his coffee like this and actually had no machines. He put large Mason jars with plastic lids on shelves and covered them with towels, preferably for over 24 hours. Deli man clearly explained that he never used metal lids, as the metal changed the taste. I had not even realized that the plastic lids were available for the jars, but they are an option and readily available. The towels are to keep the temperature consistent and let the brew steep at an even pace. I suppose it is the same concept as brewing tea in a covered teapot. This seemed a long process to go through for coffee, but quite frankly his coffee was outrageously perfect.

To this day, I only use Mason jars for cold brews and always cover my jars with a towel. Of course I have adapted the recipe and added coffee ice cubes.

INGREDIENTS

Coffee of your choice

Good water (I never use tap)

1–2 half gallon Mason jars with plastic lids

Several cotton tea bags

Towels

Ice cube trays

1. Fill 3 empty tea bags with coffee grounds and place the bags in the jar.

2. Fill the Mason jar with cold filtered water, pouring the water over the bags.

3. Cover the jar with lid, cover with towel, and let sit overnight or up to 24 hours.

4. Remove grounds by straining through a fine mesh strainer.

5. Keep in fridge and serve hot or cold. (At this point you can transfer to any pitcher you like or keep in Mason Jar.)

6. For ice cubes, fill ice cube trays with coffee and freeze. Serve with cold coffee or blend in a smoothie.

Lazy Days Nut Milk

Exactly as the title suggests, this was one of those days that I wanted a latte or smoothie but had no nut milk. I did have almond butter. So I tried this and it worked. I love it when that happens.

INGREDIENTS

1–2 Tbsp. of raw almond butter (or nut butter of your choice)

1 vanilla bean (or vanilla powder)

Pinch of salt

$1/2$ teaspoon (or more) coconut sugar (optional)

1. Put all ingredients in the blender with 1 liter of water and blend on high.

Chocolate-Peanut Butter Milk

One of my favorite flavor combinations is chocolate and peanut butter. There is perfection in the Reese's Peanut Butter Cup® that no one can replicate. It is a perfect balance of salt, sweet, and peanut butter.

This recipe can be made with or without coffee, but never without the peanut milk. Make the peanut milk in the same way as the nut milk recipe.

INGREDIENTS

$1/3$ cup peanuts

Pinch of salt

3 cups water

$1/2$ tsp. coconut oil

1 heaping Tbsp. of raw cacao powder or unsweetened cocoa

1. Put all the ingredients in a blender and blend on high until frothy.

2. Place the nut milk bag or lined strainer over another container and pour the mixture through.

3. Squeeze or press out extra liquid (you may need to do this twice).

SAME RECIPE WITH ADDITION OF COFFEE

INGREDIENTS

One large cup cold filtered coffee

$1/2$ vanilla bean

Pinch of salt

1 cup peanut milk

Handful of ice

1. Mix half the milk mixture and half the cold filtered coffee with a handful of ice.

2. Add a pinch of vanilla bean.

3. Blend on high.

4. Sprinkle top with cinnamon.

The Basic Nut Milk Recipe

Milk can be made out of practically anything. The only equipment needed is a blender and any piece of thin fabric or sieve to serve as a straining bag. I will credit Suki, my dear friend and constant collaborator, with discovering the paint-strainer bag as the most practical and inexpensive material to use as a nut milk bag. As I said, anything can make milk—oats, seeds, nuts, legumes—but not everything will taste right. The formula remains the same, but the nut or seed changes the result, depending on the flavor or the fat.

INGREDIENTS

$1/3$ cup almonds (or any nut)

3 cups water

Pinch of salt

$1/2$ tsp. coconut oil (this is a binder)

1. Put all the ingredients in a blender and blend on high until frothy.

2. Place the nut milk bag or lined strainer over another container and pour the mixture through.

3. Squeeze or press out extra liquid (you may need to do this twice).

VARIATIONS

Other flavor suggestions:

- Vanilla bean
- Maple
- Almond extract
- Peppermint extract

Thick Coconut Milkshake
with Vanilla Bean

My dear friend and soul sister Leslie has a very good life in Bali. I love going to visit her for many reasons, but waking up in the morning and having a freshly cracked coconut brought to me would have to top the list. One afternoon we made milkshakes, blending the flesh with the water. We would often toss in a papaya or mango freshly picked from one of her trees. In fact, we would blend just about anything, including coffee and chocolate. We also froze them. Because finding coconuts and palm trees can be difficult in many parts of the world (sigh), one has to improvise and, perhaps, improve.

INGREDIENTS

Water from 1 fresh coconut
OR 1 bottle coconut water
(Harmless Harvest® is my favorite)

1 large handful of raw cashews
OR 1 frozen banana

$^1/_2$ vanilla bean, split—scrape the inside "meat"
from the bean and toss in blender
(the outside of the bean can be thrown away)

1 pint raspberries

3–4 mint leaves

Juice and zest of 1 lime

1. Combine the coconut, coconut water, vanilla bean, raspberries, lime juice, zest, mint, and leaves.

2. Blend till thick and smooth.

3. Optionally, you can eat it like yogurt and pour the mixture *over* the berries (or fruit).

Vegetable Juice

There is a very lovely couple with a beautiful oasis above Tallow Beach in Byron Bay, Australia, who introduced me to a world I never knew existed. Lance, one of my main yoga teachers from that period and his beautiful wife, Susan, live on a self-contained piece of completely off-the-grid property. Their house is stunning and architecturally simple in that it's almost like a tree house, yet modern at the same time. They have their own well, grow their own vegetables, and the entire family eats mostly raw foods. Lance, Susan, and their two kids glow with health. Susan is a master at juicing. She introduced me to manipulating the juicer and experimenting with just about anything to yield a different result. Her concoctions were mostly therapeutic and didn't necessarily taste very good, but I began to understand the result in how quickly the enzymes in freshly pressed juice feed the cells of your body. It is literally medicinal, liquid sunshine. If everyone drank a vegetable juice every day, I honestly think the health of the world would improve and doctors would have less to do. I haven't jumped up on my nutritional soapbox until now, but vegetable juice is the one place where I cannot hold back.

SALAD JUICE

INGREDIENTS

1 head of romaine lettuce

1 head of kale

2–3 chard leaves
(the rainbow ones are nice)

2 tomatoes

1 lemon, sliced

1. Pass each ingredient through the juicer one at a time.

2. Strain the juice though a fine mesh strainer and serve.

WINTER TAN JUICE

INGREDIENTS

1 bunch of kale

$^1/_2$ apple (optional)

1 whole lemon (I like to keep the peel on,
but it must be washed well)

1 whole beet, cut to fit juicer

4 stalks celery OR 2 English cucumbers

1–2" piece of fresh ginger

1. Pass each ingredient through the juicer.

2. Strain the juice through a fine mesh strainer and serve.

Indian Masala Chai

Just hearing the word "chai" evokes a feeling of wistfulness in my heart. I can almost smell the deep, flavorful scent of cardamom and ginger warming over a fire in large silver barrels by the chai walas (tea makers) along the sides of the roads. On my first trip to India I found myself on a temple tour in the north with an American archeologist who had been living in the mountains of Northern India for over fifteen years. She spoke Hindi like a native and was the perfect advisor when it came to teatime. She had a talent for spotting and sniffing out the best chai spots in the most random locations. Afternoons were not complete without a warm, milky tea and an overly sweet Indian dessert. I quickly grew dependent on the spices and began to discern between a "well-blended chai" and a "packaged chai." A chai masala blend is different, depending on where you are when you taste it. The word "chai" really just means "tea" and masala means "spice blend" so it can essentially be anything your heart desires. However, there are a few flavors that make up a traditional Indian chai, like cardamom, ginger, and cinnamon. Most of those spices are used for digestion. Each spice provides many other healing properties and are all layered in for a reason—but that's what good Indian food is all about.

INGREDIENTS

2 cups water

3 cups nut milk (or any milk you desire)

3 heaping tsp. (or 4 tea bags) of black tea such as Darjeeling, Assam, or a combination of both

1-inch piece of ginger root, peeled and cut into slices

10 green cardamom pods, smashed

1 or 2 cinnamon sticks

2–3 tsp. coconut sugar

1. Crush the cardamom pods with a mortar and pestle and place in a hot pot to toast for about 15–20 seconds.

2. Add the water and bring to a slow simmer. Once it is simmering, add the milk, tealeaves (or tea bags), ginger root, cinnamon sticks, and sugar.

3. Heat on low for about 10–15 minutes, mindful never to boil the milk. If the tea is too strong, add more hot water, milk, or sugar to adjust to your taste.

VARIATIONS

For a stronger and more traditional Chai taste, add a pinch of black pepper and clove.

CHAI SPICED SMOOTHIE

Put cooled chai tea in the blender and add ice cubes. Blend on high with 1 Tbsp. molasses per two cups of chai. Drink when frothy.

Acknowledgments

I am so grateful to the multitude of people who contributed to this book by offering me a glimpse into their life by sharing a memory, a moment, a laugh, a meal, or tasting some bizarre concoction that I came up with. The love that I am blessed with and the life I have lived astounds me.

Mama, thank you for your constant curiosity and for encouraging me to do the same—and for never taking us to Disneyland! Rog & Rob, thank you for taking this journey with me, finding humor in my ever-changing eating habits, and loving me everywhere and anywhere.

Ash, thank you for eating organic, crystal-infused, grass-fed everything, even when I know you don't want to. I love you so.

Di & Suz, where to begin?! My constant cheerleaders, you encouraged me to go far and wide and keep going. Di, for all the white feathers. Suz, for making me laugh so hard my sides still hurt.

Gabs, for always reminding me of who I am. Kams, for eating it all and loving it. Suki, LYMI, MYLM. Ellianna, we ARE both writers! Peter, my mentor, teacher, and friend. I did it! Renee—ahh, Renee— what can I say? Leslie, John H., my Chapman sisters, Heather, Lorena, Frances J., Michelle, Mags. Sarah & Vishal—for insisting I come to India. Ritu and Vinay, Clauds, Organic Maxwell, Dr. Levy, Lulu—for inviting me to Rome.

My teachers Lance, Lara, Lousia (do they all begin with L?), Faeq. I am on my knees with gratitude for your guidance and direction.

My multitude of cousins Dana, Susi, Charna, Shari. Love you guys! Aunt Judy. I miss you. Auntie J., thank you—just that.

Phoebe, finally! Uncle Rob, what would my blog be without you? Rebecca Cobb, for the stunning photos. My editor Shari, you are the best! Ellen, for taking a chance. I am grateful. Cho, for pushing. Francesca, my publisher. We did it!

Source List

SWEETENERS

Brown rice syrup

Lundberg (the only truly gluten-free brown rice syrup)
Product page: www.lundberg.com/products/syrup.aspx
Contact: www.lundberg.com/Info/Contact_Us.aspx

Coconut Sugar/Palm Sugar

Big Tree Farms & Sweet Tree (tree of life)
Product page: http://bigtreefarms.com/index.php/page/product/
37/60/60
Contact page: http://bigtreefarms.com/index.php/page/menu/11

Yacon syrup

Sunfoods
Product page: www.sunfood.com/yacon-syrup-16-fl-oz-organic-
raw.html
Contact page: www.sunfood.com/pages/contact-us

Molasses

Plantation
Product page: www.alliedoldenglish.com/plantation.php
Contact page: www.alliedoldenglish.com/contact.php

Wholesome
Product page: www.wholesomesweeteners.com/brands/
Wholesome_Sweeteners/Fair_Trade_Certified_Organic_
Blackstrap_Molasses.html
Contact page: www.wholesomesweeteners.com/Customer-Contacts
.html?PHPSESSID=3841a60e975c6f35805c74c593e2aae8

Honey

Y. S. Eco Bee Farms
Product page: www.ysorganic.com/honey.html
Contact page: www.ysorganic.com/more-info.html

Maple Syrup

Shady Maple Farms
www.shady-maple.com

Coombs Family
www.coombsfamilyfarms.com

Jaggery

Taj-Agro Products
www.tajagroproducts.com/jaggery.html

SALTS

Celtic Sea Salt®

Celticseasalt.com
Product page: www.celticseasalt.com/Celtic-Sea-Salt-Fine-Ground-
C6.aspx
Contact page: www.celticseasalt.com/Contact-Us-W277C549.aspx

Saltworks
Product page: www.saltworks.us/celtic-sea-salt.html
Contact page: www.saltworks.us/contact.asp

Truffle salt, Sea salt, Sel de mer, Himalayan salt

The Spice Lab
Contact page: http://shop.thespicelab.com/contact_us.php

Maldon Salt UK
Contact page: www.maldonsalt.co.uk/Contact%20Us.html

OILS

Coconut Oil

Glaser Organic Farms (this is my favorite brand of coconut oil)
Contact page: www.glaserorganicfarms.com/contact.html

Bragg
Contact page: http://bragg.com/contact/contact.php

Raw Food World
Contact page: www.therawfoodworld.com/index.php?main_page=
  contact_us

Olive Oils (this is truly a matter of taste)

Omega nutrition
Contact page: www.omeganutrition.com/contactus.asp

365 Brand (Whole Foods)
Contact page: www.wholefoodsmarket.com/company/service.php

Barini
Contact page: www.barianioliveoil.com/contact.php

SEEDS, NUTS, AND NUT BUTTERS

Artisana (for raw tahini, raw nut butters—also coconut butters
 and other products)
Contact page: www.artisanafoods.com/contact-us

Seeds of Change
Contact page: www.seedsofchange.com/contact_us.aspx

SPICES

Frontier Natural Coop • www.frontiercoop.com/
Organic, sustainably sourced spices

Penzeys Spices • www.penzeys.com

SEAWEEDS

Maine Coast Sea Vegetables (nori, dulse, wakame, etc.)
www.seaveg.com/shop

MISO, SOY SAUCE, etc.

South River Miso Company
www.southrivermiso.com

Miyako Oriental Foods
www.coldmountainmiso.com

San-J
www.san-j.com

Eden (ume plum, ume plum vinegars, nama shoyu, tamari,
 wasabi)
www.edenfoods.com

Index

About the Author

Lora Krulak is a nutritional muse who blends culinary adventure with dietary soundness. Inspired by global flavors and exotic spices, she helps people dive into an unforgettable world of vibrant colors, vivid flavors, and luscious nutrition.

More than just a recipe re-creator, Lora focuses on giving people the tools and understanding to create a healthy, vegetable-centric lifestyle . . . without the need to become a vegetarian. By focusing on whole foods in balanced combinations, she shows people that vegetables can be sexy, exciting and, most important, delicious.

Lora obtained her BFA degree from Parson School of Design, and later went on to train at ICE Culinary Cooking School. Combining her skills in the visual and culinary arts, she became an international private nutritional chef and lifestyle coach, working at top New York restaurants, and teaching yoga. In addition, she has traveled the world—from India, Bali, and Thailand to Turkey, The Middle East Australia, and Southern Europe—and brings the stories, recipes, and cooking techniques she learned and perfected overseas to all homes.

Often called "an artist with a blender and a basket of vegetables," Lora demystifies vegetables, brings simplicity to cooking, and inspires people to make healthful eating choices. She has shared her food philosophies with national audiences on *The Rachel Ray Show, Plum TV, The Food Network,* and the National Ad Campaign for Match.Com, as well as in numerous national and international magazines such as *Spa Asia, Us* magazine, *People, The New York Post, InStyle* magazine, and *Barron's.* An active blogger, her posts appear regularly on Whole Living's Meatless Monday and have earned inclusion in the prestigious Martha Stewart Martha's Circle.

She can help anyone—even the most die-hard carnivore—develop healthy eating habits that last a lifetime.